THE PEOPLE HAVE SPOKEN

(and they are wrong)

THE PEOPLE HAVE SPOKEN

(and they are wrong)

THE CASE AGAINST DEMOCRACY

DAVID HARSANYI

REGNERY PUBLISHING
Washington, DC • Since 1947

Cataloging-in-Publication data on file with the Library of Congress

ISBN 978-1-62157-202-2

Published in the United States by
Regnery Publishing, Inc.
One Massachusetts Avenue NW
Washington, DC 20001
www.Regnery.com

Manufactured in the United States of America

10 9 8 7 6 5 4 3 2 1

Books are available in quantity for promotional or premium use. Write to Director of Special Sales, Regnery Publishing, Inc., One Massachusetts Avenue NW, Washington, DC 20001, for information on discounts and terms, or call (202) 216-0600.

Distributed to the trade by
Perseus Distribution
250 West 57th Street
New York, NY 10107

For Leah and Adira

CONTENTS

Democracy: a government of the masses. Authority derived through mass meeting or any other form of "direct" expression. Results, in mobocracy. Attitude toward property is communistic . . . negating property rights. Attitude toward law is that the will of a majority shall regulate, whether it is based upon deliberation or governed by passion, prejudice, and impulse, without restraint or regard to consequences. Result is demogogism, license, agitation, discontent, anarchy.
—U.S. ARMY OFFICIAL TRAINING MANUAL NO. 2000-25
(1928–1932)

I'll keep that in mind, Mr. Bailey, when this becomes a democracy.
—STAR TREK ("THE CORBOMITE MANEUVER," 1966)

CHAPTER 1

A PLEA FOR REASON

*"On its world, the people are people. The leaders are lizards.
The people hate the lizards and the lizards rule the people."*
"Odd," said Arthur, "I thought you said it was a democracy."
"I did," said Ford. "It is."
*"So," said Arthur, hoping he wasn't sounding ridiculously obtuse,
"why don't the people get rid of the lizards?"*
*"It honestly doesn't occur to them," said Ford. "They've all got the
vote, so they all pretty much assume that the government they've
voted in more or less approximates to the government they want."*
"You mean they actually vote for the lizards?"
"Oh yes," said Ford with a shrug, "of course."
"But," said Arthur, going for the big one again, "why?"
*"Because if they didn't vote for a lizard," said Ford,
"the wrong lizard might get in."*
—Douglas Adams, *So Long, and Thanks for All the Fish*

I f you're going to write a book critical of one of the most admired ideas ever concocted by mankind, it's probably important that you appropriately define the subject matter. So, for the most concise description of this book's target, I turn to the popular user-generated, hyper-democratized online encyclopedia *Wikipedia*—a place where consensus typically decides truth.

"Democracy," according to the masses at *Wikipedia*, "is a form of government in which all eligible citizens have an equal say in the decisions that affect their lives. Democracy allows eligible citizens to participate equally—either directly or through elected representatives—in the proposal, development, and creation of laws. It encompasses social, economic and cultural conditions that enable the free and equal practice of political self-determination."[1]

This is more or less the standard portrayal of democracy, one that most Americans (at least those who spend much time pondering these sorts of issues) would accept as true. And, as this book will contend, half of this definition is unqualified gibberish and the other half, while true, is a decidedly dangerous truth. For starters, "democracy," as embedded in our national consciousness, functions under an array of fictions.

No, "democracy" is not interchangeable or synonymous with the ideas of "freedom" or "liberalism."

No, majoritarian rule is not inherently more moral, or more useful, or more virtuous than the decisions of one person or of a minority.

No, democracy does not give us equal say in the decisions that affect our lives, as *Wikipedia* would have it. The more democracy grows, the less say we have, actually.

No, the opposite of democracy is not tyranny; in fact, as America's Founders knew, democracy itself can be tyrannical, which is why the Constitution has safeguards against it at every turn.

No, democracy doesn't always temper extremism (it can fan it) or create transparency.

Democracy doesn't preserve or expand cultural or intellectual diversity, as its very purpose is to run the state on widespread conformity.

Democracy isn't a counterweight to the concentrated powers of the elites. As the Greeks knew, democracies are prey to demagogues. Elites routinely manipulate democracies, because it's not hard to manipulate a crowd.

No, democracy doesn't create economic and cultural freedom; it's more often the other way around.

Actually, democracy is, by any reasonable standard, the most overrated, overused, overvalued, and misunderstood idea in political life. We have way too much of it. We *think* way too much of it. These days, an honest observer of Washington politics must concede that democracy has made our government irrational, invasive, and irresponsible. It has offered the American people two methods of governance: majoritarian domination or complete dysfunction (though many in Washington confuse healthy gridlock and unhealthy dysfunction). It deals in corrupt incentives, encourages a mob mentality, and in the process undermines the virtues that sustain a healthy republic. It has left a large traditionalist minority—those most wedded to America's founding, constitutional ideals——dispirited, as they see their country apparently hijacked by a new revolutionary majority that believes in the power of "the people" rather than constitutional restraint and gradualist reform. It has put all fifty states, once marginally independent, at the mercy of an ever-growing centralized government in Washington, resting on national majority rule that dictates everything from healthcare policy to education policy. And when a national majority, through the power of the federal government, can overrule majorities in the several states or in localities, it is no wonder that many people feel powerless, because national majoritarian decisions cannot take into account endlessly varied local conditions, contexts, and information. Rarely can they take into account subtle, sophisticated, and substantive arguments. So, in turn, national democracy encourages us to be lazy, to do less thinking, to accept bumper sticker slogans as policy, to be less individualistic and less educated about the world around us, and it encourages others to take advantage of our lethargy; it allows the most powerful to abuse that power.

Yet in America today it is considered a truism that democracy is the supreme form of government. Questioning democracy's pristine moral standing will get you labeled an imperialist, monarchist, fascist, or worse (if you can imagine such a thing). Though oddly enough there is increasing suspicion, against our own democratic instincts and prejudices, that maybe democracy is not the best export, after all, to the Arab or Islamic worlds. Maybe it is not a universal panacea.

While disparaging democracy seems unsavory, it's nothing new. Democracy is one of the most debated topics in the history of political philosophy. At the core of the debate are fundamental questions that no one really asks anymore. Some of these are deep, like: What is the essence of human nature? Others are more prosaic, like: What the hell is the purpose of government? To make sure you buckle up when you drive? To set up your retirement fund with a one-percent return? To ensure your happiness? To subsidize your birth control? To limit the size of your cola? To make sure you do not ingest trans fats?

In popular American debate, these political questions are most often boiled down into two questions: Do you want more government or do you want less government?—though some who want more (government funding for abortions, say) represent it as less while those who want less (no subsidized contraception, perhaps) are represented as wanting more (a national "war on women," no less). No doubt, less versus more is an important debate—I've spent my career arguing about it—but it's not the only one.

In classical political philosophy, government's purpose is to cultivate virtue in its citizens. For Aristotle and Augustine, Plato and Aquinas, Edmund Burke and Alasdair MacIntyre, a state's success is not measured solely by wealth, power, influence, or the size of its welfare state or its military, but more by the virtue of its members. By virtue, philosophers mean the universally accepted good qualities of people. Virtue is not inherent nor is it a temporary passion like anger or empathy. It is something we obtain through practice and lose through neglect. A healthy state doesn't need to coerce people to virtue (which would be impossible, even if it wanted to), but it has a responsibility to create the environment that allows virtue to thrive.

For many of the Founders, the purpose of the state was to enforce a very few rules that guaranteed a stable government, that dispersed political power, that set out the conditions for material prosperity, and that focused on individual freedom. And they put in place protections against a direct national democracy—such as the electoral college, the indirect election of senators, different terms for senators and congressmen, the many powers reserved to the states—because there was no widespread liberty to pursue happiness in an undifferentiated national mob.

Today, we are moving away from a diffused representative republic. When liberals crusade to dismantle the electoral college or scoff at states' rights or prohibit Senate filibusters, they are fighting for a more centralized democracy in which liberty becomes susceptible to the fleeting whims of the majority, who can determine what your healthcare looks like, what your children should be taught, and what marriage should be. Is that really any of *their* business? The fact that it isn't is why majoritarianism is imbued with a morality it doesn't deserve. When movements like Occupy Wall Street claim (falsely, as it turns out) to represent the "99 percent," they assume that the larger the majority, the more right it is. That is an assertion without a well-articulated moral philosophy behind it. It is, in fact, the morality of a lynch mob. Conservatives can be just as guilty of this too, when they go into rhapsodies about the American people and how power should be returned to them. But "the people" are not the source, or the reliable protector, of our freedom. We already defer too much power to other people. When "the people" have power, it takes only 51 percent of them to ban a stiff energy drink or a decent light bulb—a crime against not only liberty but decent luminosity. It's not an accident that the whole design of the Constitution is for a limited federal government, restricting the ability of "the people," in a national majority, from interfering with the rights and freedoms of individuals and the several states. It is "the people," through the federal government, who have been rolling back those restrictions. It is "the people," through the federal government, who have empowered the bullying by the nanny state. It is "the people," through the federal government, who have figured out that they can get "benefits" paid for by others, which is perhaps the biggest corruption of all. As Alexander Fraser Tyler is said to have noted, "A democracy cannot exist as a permanent form of government. It can only exist until the majority discovers it can vote itself largess out of the public treasury. After that, the majority always votes for the candidate promising the most benefits with the result the democracy collapses because of the loose fiscal policy ensuing, always to be followed by a dictatorship, then a monarchy."

Yes, it's been a lot better to live in a democracy than under tyrannical one-party rule. Democracy has been more moral than communist rule. It has been a better choice than fascist regimes. When judging world history, in fact, we can safely assert that human beings who have lived under democratic systems have enjoyed a safer, more virtuous, and more prosperous existence than any other form of government.

But there is no guarantee that our democracy will remain that way unless we understand why it's worked for us, why it's no longer working for us, and why it can't work for others. Democracy, after all, is only as good as the society it rests on. That is why John Adams, in an oft-quoted line, said, "Our Constitution was made only for a moral and religious people. It is wholly inadequate to the government of any other."[2] He meant a certain kind of morality, a certain kind of religion, the kind in which the American people had been raised and in which the principles of free government, of a republic, made sense and could be sustained. You don't have to be a believer to believe history's lesson. Not all societies have that, and even those that have it can lose it. As the political philosopher Roger Scruton reminds us, many of the virtues we like to associate with democracy actually precede democracy and are not guaranteed by democracy:

> Democracy was introduced into Russia without any adequate protection for human rights. And many human rights were protected in 19th Century Britain long before the emergence of anything that we would call democracy. In the Middle East today, we find parties standing for election, like the Muslim Brotherhood in Egypt, which regards an electoral victory as the opportunity to crush dissent and impose a way of life that for many citizens is simply unacceptable. In such circumstances democracy is a threat to human rights and not a way of protecting them.[3]

When democracy yields good things it is not because good things are *inherent* to the process of democracy, it is because good things are byproducts of our own ethics and morality and good sense. More important than the process of democracy is a respect for individual freedom, the rule of law, economic freedom, freedom of religion and speech, and a belief in dividing political power. If democracy sustains these, then good things will result, but the process of democracy can just as easily curtail them. An astute, moral, benevolent dictator could just as easily guide humanity to an enlightened, free, moral, and prosperous future. But the chance of an astute, moral, benevolent dictator existing is only slightly less than a similarly inclined mob.

"America is a republic not a democracy!" is something you hear quite often in conservative circles. But that too, is shorthand of a kind. A republic is a form of government in which the state is the concern of democratically elected officials. The directness or indirectness of representation is not what makes a republic but the lack of a hereditary monarch. The modern United Kingdom, therefore, is both a democracy and a monarchy, but it's not a republic. The United States is a democratic republic. For our purposes, any mention of the American "republic" will intimate that we're talking about a diffused democratic state, where checks and balances of all kinds have been erected to blunt the power of the far-reaching majority. John Dunn, a historian of democracy, explains the distinction in his book *Democracy: A History*: "A representative government differed decisively from a democracy not in the fundamental structure of authority which underlay it, but in the institutional mechanisms which directed its course and helped keep it in being over time."

Not that I'm pulling punches. This book will condemn democracy—in any form—as a false idol and a clumsy system that corrodes freedom and prosperity. It is, at best, a necessary evil to be used sparingly. Our nation puts far too much value on the value of a vote, and far too little on the value of liberty. It is not democracy we should be praising, not a process, but the philosophical traditions of natural law and classical liberalism. With them, when people understand and believe in their principles, a republic can flourish. Without them, democracy can lead us down a very different path. Unfortunately, it's the path we're on now.

PART I

THE MOB

...the mother of tyrants.
—DIOGENES

CHAPTER 2

I DON'T
TRUST YOU PEOPLE

Anti-intellectualism has been a constant thread winding its way through our political and cultural life, nurtured by the false notion that democracy means that "my ignorance is just as good as your knowledge."
—Isaac Asimov, "A Cult of Ignorance"

The majority is never right. Never, I tell you! That's one of these lies in society that no free and intelligent man can ever help rebelling against. Who are the people that make up the biggest proportion of the population—the intelligent ones or the fools? I think we can agree it's the fools, no matter where you go in this world, it's the fools that form the overwhelming majority.
—Henrik Ibsen, An Enemy of the People

Creating and maintaining a state that governs serious matters of life and death, of justice and security, of war and peace, requires both wisdom and knowledge. Can anyone honestly say that most politicians possess these qualities—much less most people?

Winston Churchill supposedly remarked that the best argument against democracy is a five-minute discussion with the average voter. Alas, it's difficult to argue. That's exactly why, unlike many of my more tolerant fellow citizens, I have little confidence in the ability of the electorate to make sensible decisions for me, for my country, or for themselves. I don't say that because the political tide isn't going my way (though it rarely does) or because I find the worldview of most Americans disagreeable (I often do). I base my skepticism on certain incontrovertible truths that emerge from a multitude of social studies and overwhelming empirical evidence. So should you.

If we're to make collective national choices, what people know and what they think they know matters. And before we can begin to understand how unlikely most voters are to make rational choices even when they're equipped with intelligence and information, we have to concede that many, if not most, voters are unprepared even to try. If democracies operated the way their proponents say they do, most of us would feel compelled to pay more attention to history, civics, and current events, because politics intrudes on more of life than ever. But we don't. Rather than take advantage of the extraordinary accessibility of information, in all mediums, we abandon our judgment to the pithiest platitudes and the most exaggerated promises. Some scholars have argued that anywhere between 25 and 35 percent of the public lack the knowledge to make the most elementary electoral choices. And that figure has not decreased with technological advances.

The political IQ of "low-information voters" (admittedly, a condescending euphemism usually applied to those with whom one disagrees, which I will refrain from using hereafter) is not the most corrosive problem with democracy. You can be fully informed about the world and still make dreadful choices anyway. We all do. Collectivizing those choices and then coercing everyone to participate is what makes democratizing all decisions a terrible idea. And what happens when you even lack the most basic knowledge of history and civics? Your vote will be bad news for the rest of us. This seems obvious. Yet to declare publicly that you believe some people don't have the capacity to make healthy political judgments for everyone is, in America, tantamount to committing blasphemy. Such an opinion seems judgmental, elitist, and discriminatory.

It is all those things. It's also true. Does anyone believe that every citizen does his best to educate himself and then vote in the best interest of the nation, rather than in the best interest of himself? If too many of us were to admit that some votes are less worthy than others, it would blow up the foundational idea that a relatively wealthy and educated citizenry will most often make the right communal choices. Let's be clear: to contend that all votes are not equally valuable is not to say that some people are "better" than others. No one is obliged to be educated about labor policy or foreign policy or any other policy. A person who studies architecture is not a better human being than the person who studies theoretical physics or filmmaking, but he is certainly more prepared to weigh in on what my new house should look like.

There are many kinds of voters to distrust: the uninformed, the uneducated, the crazy, the uninterested. But the worst are people who believe they know everything. The scope of the problem is apparent every time we browse through our emails, watch cable news television, listen to celebrities, and hang out at block parties with our neighbors: We're confronted with fiercely stupid theories from people who are exceptionally sure of themselves. People I once respected—folks whose intellects and accomplishments soar above my own—aren't shy about asserting that the economy is controlled by a half-dozen shadowy corporations or that Barack Obama is a Manchurian candidate with a Bangladeshi birth certificate tucked under his pillow.

We may laugh off these nutty ideas, but in a democracy they have consequences. One-third of Americans, for instance, believe in UFOs[1]—a number that's up 15 percent since the 1980s. A Harris poll from a few years back found that 28 percent of us believe in witches, and 40 percent of the public—46 percent of women—believe that ghosts are hovering in the so-called "real" world. Over 20 percent of us think we've actually seen a poltergeist, and about 30 percent of Americans believe that a person's character and personality quirks are predetermined by the alignment of stars and planets observable from earth at the moment of his birth.[2] A few years later, the same poll showed those numbers going up, with 42 percent of Americans believing in ghosts (a particularly strong belief among younger Americans), 36 percent believing in creationism and UFOs, 29 percent believing in astrology, 26 percent in witches, and 24 percent that they were once another person.[3] And we're supposed to care what these folks think about the optimal top marginal tax rate?[4]

Occam's razor, a principle of logic, tells us that among competing explanations, the simplest is to be preferred. When it comes to politics, however, countless Americans disregard such reasoning. I fear for my country not only because I spy the occasional "Bush Knew!" bumper sticker decomposing on a Prius in my neighborhood but also because a staggering Scripps Howard poll a few years back found that one in three Americans believes the 9/11 attacks might have been an inside job. After all, why would a bunch of Islamic radicals want to inflict a massive terror attack on the United States' financial capital? It's gotta be something else, right? But it doesn't end there.

According to a 2013 Public Policy poll:

- 51 percent *of voters*—not simply Americans, but those who bother to vote—say a larger conspiracy was at work in the assassination of President Kennedy.
- 21 percent of voters say a UFO crashed in Roswell, New Mexico, in 1947 and that the U.S. government covered it up.
- 28 percent of voters believe a secretive elite with a globalist agenda is conspiring to establish an authoritarian world government.
- 15 percent of voters think the medical and pharmaceutical industries "invent" new diseases to make money.

A Fairleigh Dickinson University PublicMind poll in early 2013 found that 63 percent of registered voters believe in at least one of the following conspiracy theories: President Bush knew about the planned 9/11 attacks in advance, President Obama is hiding information about his birth and early life, Republicans stole the 2004 presidential election through voter fraud in Ohio, and Democrats stole the 2012 presidential election through voter fraud.[5] (The silver lining in that poll, of course, is that it might make us trust democracy a little less.)

Our society, in fact, is surprisingly accepting of these superstitions. Remember how much time the mainstream media devoted to conspiracy theories in their coverage of the fiftieth anniversary of the Kennedy assassination. Our history is filled with consequential events that never happened but still shape our understanding of the world. Richard Hofstadter drew attention to this conspiratorial strain in his 1965 book, *The Paranoid Style in American Politics*, though for the most part he limited his analysis to the right end of the political spectrum. More recently Jesse Walker, in *The United States of Paranoia*, has demonstrated the bipartisan appeal of conspiratorial thinking:

> Pundits tend to write off political paranoia as a feature of the fringe, a disorder that occasionally flares up until the sober center can put out the flames. They're wrong. The fear of conspiracies has been a potent force across the political spectrum, from the colonial era to the present, in the establishment as well as the extremes. Conspiracy theories played major roles in the conflicts from the Indian War of the seventeen century to labor battles of the Gilded Age, from the Civil War to the Cold War, from the American Revolution to the War on Terror.

Over the last couple of centuries, substantial numbers of Americans have believed that President Zachary Taylor was poisoned by his wife, that Andrew Jackson staged an assassination attempt to curry sympathy from voters, that Franklin D. Roosevelt knew about the attack on Pearl Harbor in advance and let it happen so he could fight World War II, that the CIA sold crack in impoverished neighborhoods, and that gays poisoned the population with AIDS. And if you've had an email account the past fifteen years, you've heard that George W. Bush refused to sell his Dallas home to blacks and that Barack Obama was sworn into office on the Koran. There are thousands of examples of misleading and completely untrue stories about presidents, and they spread quickly. We tend to believe these stories if they reinforce our existing aversion to a politician.

These conspiracy theories matter because people who believe in one of them will believe in others, and at some point they're going to believe something that matters at the ballot box—even if the Koch Brothers *are* sabotaging those voting machines. Science fiction writer Alan Moore once wrote, "The truth is, that it is not the Jewish banking conspiracy or the grey aliens or the 12 foot reptiloids from another dimension that are in control. The truth is more frightening, nobody is in control."[6] In turbulent times (and really, they all seem turbulent when we have to live through them, no?) people feel a lack of control. Polls show that we say we want all kinds of things, that we desire change and improvement, but most often people crave stability. Gita Johar, a professor at the Columbia Business School, recently explained to *Wired* magazine that increasingly, once-normal, rational adults are turning to psychics for guidance. "You have an illusion then that you can then control the outcome," she explains. "People want the illusion of control."[7] And surely, Americans are feeling that they are progressively losing control (or losing the perception that they ever had control) of the economy; the world is spiraling in unpredictable directions, and our personal futures are often nebulous. The idea that we can control outcomes is one of the most dangerous fantasies we operate under, yet it drives much of our political debate.

At one time Art Bell's *Coast to Coast*, devoted to the "paranormal," was America's highest-rated late-night radio talk show, with five hundred stations and 15 million listeners. Today Alex Jones, a radio host who ferreted out government conspiracies behind the Sandy Hook school shooting, the Oklahoma City bombing, and the moon landing, produces movies like *The 9/11 Chronicles: Truth Rising* and *Invisible Empire: A New World Order Defined*, with audiences in the millions. He has almost 545,000 subscribers to his YouTube page and broadcasts news twenty-four hours a day from a high-tech TV studio. His website, Infowars.com, has around 2 million unique visitors every month, rivaling many of the more well-known sites on the internet. Thanks to communications technology, we're no longer talking about a bunch of boobs meeting in a cellar and rationing Tang. These days conspiracies like "false flag" attacks (covert operations conducted by governments and corporations that appear to be carried out by other entities like terrorist groups) constitute an alternative reality.

Kooks don't run our democracy yet, but they have a bigger say than most of us imagine. We dismiss them at our own risk. Outside of politics it's easy to see how they can be dangerous. When millions of parents refuse to vaccinate their children because a few celebrities and medical quacks have told them that vaccines are related to autism, we face local outbreaks of diseases we thought had been contained. Millions of supposedly rational human beings are willing to believe, without a shred of evidence, that genetically modified foods are a dangerous corporate plot against consumers, hindering a new technology that could save billions of dollars and millions of lives. Likewise, crazy ideas invade the political environment.

There is probably little we can do about the crazy or gullible—though their sheer numbers tell us that silliness permeates the democratic process. The man who believes a papal cabal is pumping fluoride into our water supply has a vote that cancels out yours, but more damage is done by the citizen who doesn't care enough to inform himself but does care enough to vote.

"A popular government without popular information or the means of acquiring it is but a Prologue to Farce or Tragedy, or, perhaps both," James Madison wrote, and "a people who mean to be their own Governors, must arm themselves with the power which knowledge gives."[8] Are we making decisions based on the information we need? Of course not. Michael X. Delli Carpini, the dean of the Annenberg School for Communication at the University of Pennsylvania, concludes that a steady decline in civic knowledge since World War II has left "slightly under 1 percent" of American voters fully prepared to exercise their franchise. The electorate's knowledge has barely improved since the 1930s, says Ilya Somin, a professor of law at George Mason University who studies democracy and political knowledge. In a poll conducted a month after the historic Republican takeover of the House of Representatives in 1994, for instance, less than half of Americans had ever heard of Newt Gingrich, the focus of nearly every news outlet in the months leading up to the election. At the height of the Cold War, in 1964, only 34 percent knew that the Soviet Union wasn't a member of NATO. And a 2002 study found that 35 percent of Americans believe that the phrase "From each according to his ability, to each according to his need" could be found in the Constitution. (Not yet!)

How could this be? The average citizen is no less *capable* today of understanding how government works than he was back in the old days. Generally speaking, we're probably smarter. IQ test scores in the United States increased by an average of three points every decade of the twentieth century. When measured on an unadjusted scale, IQ scores today are about twenty points above those of three generations ago. In the lingo of the tests, your grandparents were a "dull normal" while you are likely "bright normal." Congratulations.

And we're certainly not lacking *access* to information. A person can look up a bible verse or a mathematical equation or a famous speech on his smartphone at any time of the day or night. There are thousands of websites with sourced material, offering every viewpoint on every issue. Some Americans yearn for the days of three network newscasts, believing that the "impartial" media made for a healthier democracy. Too many choices lead us astray, they argue. But it's unlikely that people were better informed in the past, and the press has never been impartial—certainly not the Big Three evening news broadcasts from the 1940s to the 1990s.

It's true that in the internet age our collective interests have atomized, but individually they've become hyper-focused. We know a lot more about the things we care about. Our media are, as they say, "democratized" (and democratized media, unlike democratized government, benefit consumers by enhancing the range of choices). We may be more proficient and more engaged in many aspects of the world around us. And with all that competition for our attention, who's going to want to read about tax reform proposals?

Allan Bloom famously argued in *The Closing of the American Mind* (1987) that "higher education has failed democracy and impoverished the souls of today's students," but the problem appears to begin long before college. Americans' understanding of basic civics has almost certainly diminished over the last hundred years. In 2013, an eighth-grade examination from 1912 turned up in a dusty attic and was donated to the Bullitt County History Museum in Kentucky. It made its way online, where it went "viral," enabling browsers to compare their own knowledge with their great-grandparents'.[9] The exam covers eight subjects in which thirteen-year-old students were expected to be proficient. Here's a sampling:

Arithmetic

Write in words the following: .5764; .000003; .123416; 653.0965; 43.37.

Solve: 35.7 plus 4.

At $1.62½ a cord, what will be the cost of a pile of wood 24 ft. long, 4 ft. wide, and 6 ft. 3 in. high?

Grammar

Define proper noun; common noun. Name the properties of a noun.

What is a Personal Pronoun? Decline I.

Adjectives have how many Degrees of Comparison? Compare good; wise; beautiful.

Geography

Locate Erie Canal; what waters does it connect, and why is it important?

Locate the following countries which border each other: Turkey, Greece, Servia, Montenegro, and Roumania.

Locate these cities: Mobile. Quebec, Buenos Aires, Liverpool, Honolulu.

Physiology

How does the liver compare in size with other glands in the human body? Where is it located? What does it secrete?

Where is the chief nervous center of the body?

Define Cerebrum; Cerebellum.

Civil Government

Name and define the three branches of the government of the United States.

Give three duties of the President. What is meant by the veto power?

Name three rights given Congress by the Constitution and two rights denied Congress.

History

Who first discovered the following places—Florida, Pacific Ocean, Miss[issippi] River, St Lawrence River?
Describe the battle of Quebec.
Name 2 presidents who have died in office: three who were assas[s]inated.

Now, this isn't a terribly difficult test, though there are questions that could trip anyone up. But are you confident that 50 percent of voters could answer at least five of the questions correctly? 30 percent? 20 percent? You'll notice that much of the test is concerned with history, geography, and civics. When *Newsweek* asked a thousand voters to take America's official citizenship test a few years back, 29 percent couldn't name the vice president of the United States. The same poll revealed that 73 percent of voters couldn't identify our opponent in the Cold War, 44 percent were unable to define the Bill of Rights, and 6 percent couldn't find Independence Day on a calendar. A Marist poll found that 26 percent had no idea whom the United States had declared independence from—6 percent thought we had revolted from various other nations, among them France, China, Japan, Mexico, or Spain.[10]

The National Assessment of Educational Progress is a nationally representative and continuing assessment of American elementary and secondary students' academic achievement. A study of NAEP results by the Pioneer Institute for Public Policy found widespread poor performance in history and civics—a result that "portends a decay of the knowledge, skills, and dispositions needed for a lifetime of active, engaged citizenship." Most of the hand-wringing over American education is concerned with math, science, and reading, but 35 percent of eighth-graders scored proficient or higher in math, and 34 percent did so in reading and science.[11] Only 22 percent reached the proficient level in civics, and only 18 percent did so in U.S. history. Why is history important in a democracy? Walter A. McDougall, a Pulitzer Prize–winning historian, explains:

> The first, obviously, is its intellectual function. History is the grandest vehicle for vicarious experience: it educates provincial young minds (we are all born provincial) and obliges them to reason, wonder, and brood about the vastness, richness, and tragedy of the human condition. If taught well, history trains young minds in the rules of evidence and logic, teaches them how to approximate truth through the patient exposure of falsehood. That is, no one can claim to have a lock on historical Truth with a capital T, but rigorous history should teach us what is False with a capital F. History also gives children the mental trellis they need to situate themselves in time and space and organize all other knowledge they acquire in the humanities and sciences. To deny students history is to alienate them from their community, nation, culture, and species.

Further cause for concern comes from a survey by the McCormick Tribune Freedom Museum, which found that only one in four Americans was able to name one of the five fundamental freedoms guaranteed by the First Amendment (freedom of speech, religion, the press, and assembly, and the right to petition for redress of grievances). A majority could remember that the First Amendment guarantees freedom of speech but little more. Researchers threw in some other "freedoms" to see if people thought they too were mentioned in the First Amendment. One in five respondents agreed "the right to own and raise pets" was guaranteed by the First Amendment, and one in five agreed that driving was guaranteed. When 55 percent of American adults believe that "education" is a right guaranteed by the Constitution but only 24 percent understand that the First Amendment protects the free exercise of religion, we shouldn't be surprised by some of the bitter debates that Washington faces.

It's not all a lost cause, because we do know some things. Four out of ten citizens could, on the other hand, name two of the three *American Idol* judges at the time, as well as the main characters from *The Simpsons*—and 52 percent could name two of them. There is absolutely nothing wrong with that. The problem is that while 22 percent of Americans polled could name all the members of the Simpson family, only one in a thousand surveyed could name all five freedoms granted under the First Amendment. In this democracy, where every vote is treated as sacred, 74 percent of those polled by Zogby could name all Three Stooges, but only 42 could name all three branches of government.

According to the Annenberg Public Policy Center, even fewer Americans (38 percent) could name all three branches of the U.S. government: the executive, legislative, and judicial branches. Hardly half of Americans know that a two-thirds majority vote by Congress is needed to overturn a presidential veto. Only 37 percent knew that a citizen cannot appeal a Supreme Court decision to the Federal Court of Appeals. Only 62 percent knew that the U.S. Supreme Court carries the responsibility for determining the constitutionality of legislation. Fewer than half of Americans knew that split decisions in the Supreme Court have the same effect as 9-0 ones.

Is this ignorance of history and civics new? Probably not. In 1960, scholars at the University of Michigan published *The American Voter*, the first data-driven study of voting habits based on election survey results. The study proved that American voters were, generally speaking, uninformed and disorganized thinkers, lacking intellectual curiosity about why they themselves and others voted as they did. Most voters, the study found, cast their ballot based principally on party identifications, which were inherited from parents. Moreover, the study found that the "independent" voters—moderates in today's parlance—were even less conscientious about the politics of the day than the partisans.

Other scholars have debated the findings of *The American Voter* for years. Voters, some say, have become more sophisticated, and ideological realignments prove that the findings of *The American Voter* are antiquated. Yet subsequent studies, in the 1970s and 2000s, have reached similar conclusions. We haven't gotten any more curious about politics, though the consequences of self-rule have gotten a lot more substantial.

CHAPTER 3

THE HORRIBLE TRUTH ABOUT WASHINGTON

(is that we don't know the horrible truth)

Lisa, the whole reason we have elected officials is so we don't have to think all the time. Just like that rain forest scare a few years back: our officials saw there was a problem and they fixed it, didn't they?
—HOMER SIMPSON, "BART'S COMET"

I could see how "democracy" might do very well in a society of saints and sages led by an Alfred or an Antoninus Pius. Short of that, I was unable to see how it could come to anything but an ochlocracy of mass-men led by a sagacious knave. The collective capacity for bringing forth any other outcome seemed simply not there.
—ALBERT NOCK, *MEMOIRS OF A SUPERFLUOUS MAN*

It's difficult for democracy to function properly under the most favorable circumstances, but it has no chance at all when millions of voters are divorced from objective reality and incapable of understanding what is going on in Washington. It is certainly a personal fault and detrimental for any representative government not to understand the most basic working of the country you live in. But there's nothing particularly appalling about failing to comprehend the massively complicated legislation that makes its way through Congress.

Bold ideas move people. Big ideas seduce them. And nothing crushes passion like a decimal point. Few things get politicians into more trouble than offering voters too many details. Yet every election cycle, pundits of all denominations join to lament the fact that candidates aren't putting enough meat on their platitudes. Let's be honest: in politics, details can equal disaster. Whereas wonks and columnists might eat up charts and white papers, the electorate has better things to do—most notably any activity not entailing looking at a chart or reading a white paper. That is why we function under a representative democracy rather than under a 300 million–person bull session. Voters, busy with real life, operate under the assumption that the people they send to Washington own calculators, watched enough *Schoolhouse Rock!* to know how a bill becomes a law and, in some broad sense, share their worldview.

There is an impression in Washington that the longer a document is, the more it says. Major political parties should also understand that some things are simply assumed by voters. Take the Ten Commandments, the gold standard of political platforms. God commands: thou shalt not commit adultery. He doesn't instruct the Israelites to break out into subcommittees to haggle over the definition of a "neighbor's wife" before the law is carved into stone. They get the gist. The Declaration of Independence is a one-pager, and it covers the aspirations of freedom for all of mankind. Mitt Romney's 2012 "Believe in America" economic plan has fifty-nine policy proposals and 156 endnotes. Trust me; no one's ever grabbed a musket to defend an endnote.

Who has the time or attention span? The electorate will never be more interested in tax reform than it is in *Dancing with the Stars* or *Call of Duty*. I don't think that voters should be fixated on public policy. In a healthy republic, they wouldn't have to worry every waking hour about what their government is doing.

The more localized and tightly focused a law is, the more likely Americans are to understand it. But the problems that the federal government tries to deal with are now terribly complex, as are the resulting large-scale collective measures that try to coerce the entire nation into participation (and that no one understands, not even the congressmen who voted for them). Trying to deal with the anxieties and problems of over 300 million citizens rather than one municipality or state, these laws are often intrusive yet ineffectual.

The *Federal Register*, published since 1936, is the daily diary of federal agencies' rules, notices, and other acts. The first yearly volume of the *Federal Register* came to 2,620 pages. The 2012 volume filled 78,961 pages.[1] On average, Washington adds 286 pages every workday. In one randomly selected week in 2013, agencies published eighty-four new final rules and added 1,412 new pages. If a rule costs more than $100 million in a given year, it is deemed "economically significant." 2012 saw the publication of nearly thirty "economically significant" rules. The Competitive Enterprise Institute, a free-market think tank, estimates that the total burden of these regulations reaches $1.8 trillion per year.[2] Newton was able to distill the rules of physics within the 974 pages of his *Principia Mathematica*, and God himself confined his rather detailed code of life to the two hundred pages of the Torah. But the Affordable Care Act, better known as Obamacare, has produced over *eleven thousand* pages of regulations.[3] And we're only getting started.

In a highly centralized and hyper-regulatory government like ours, no one really knows what is going on. The electorate can't possibly make informed choices, and even their elected representatives don't have the time to understand more than the basics of most legislation. In the midst of all this ignorance, voters become perilously susceptible to fearmongering, misinformation, and blind partisanship. This isn't exactly a new state of affairs, but the problem has become acute.

It's easy to appreciate this danger when you consider how diffuse the costs of government have become. Take taxes—the very impetus for revolution. Most of our tax burden is hidden. Not one American in a hundred could make an accurate estimate of how much he truly pays, not just in income and sales taxes—how many people keep track of the total sales tax they pay each year?—but in pass-through taxes imposed on corporations and collected from consumers with higher prices. Throw in the magical dollars conjured from thin air by deficit spending, and you've got a population largely numb to the cost of government.

On the other hand, the benefits are very obvious to the people who receive them. In a true democracy, the opposition to government spending would be diffuse and unfocused, while the people who benefit from the State's largesse would be highly motivated. You don't need 51 percent of the vote to loot the public treasury in a pure democracy. You can do it with an energized 30 or 40 percent, provided the opposition does not unite and organize to stop them. Judge Janice Rogers Brown was on target when she said, "A democracy is inevitably transformed into a kleptocracy."

Let's consider one of the most contentious issues of the past few years, the "debt ceiling." The debate over raising the debt ceiling in the autumn of 2013 was spectacularly partisan, yet few Americans had any idea what it was all about. Both sides encouraged false conceptions about the debt ceiling to gain political traction. Why wouldn't they? When the debate began, twice as many Americans believed that raising the limit meant authorizing more borrowing "for future expenditures" than believed (correctly) that it meant "paying off the debts [Washington] has already accumulated."[4]

The misunderstanding predominated in every segment of American society—millennials, Gen Xers, and baby boomers; the poor and the rich; the educated and the uneducated—all were wrong.

To be fair, lifting the debt ceiling without securing comparable savings in the future—which is what Republicans were asking for—was the equivalent of creating future debt. Democrats, who wanted the ceiling lifted without any conditions, exploited the public's ignorance, convincing them that Republicans proposed "defaulting" on the national debt. That wasn't true—the federal government simply would have prioritized debt payments and cut elsewhere.

The most famous legislation of recent decades is Obamacare. Although many people appeared to have strong opinions on this landmark act, only a few had even the slightest understanding of it. It wasn't only Democratic or Republican partisans who failed to understand Obamacare, but the very people whom the law was supposed to help most—the uninsured. A *Wall Street Journal*/NBC News poll from September 2013 found that 76 percent of uninsured persons "didn't understand the law and how it would affect them." Three years after the law's passage—after heavy and favorable coverage in the media and the expenditure of hundreds of millions of dollars on a PR campaign—only 32 percent of the uninsured said they were "fairly" or "very" likely to get coverage through Obamacare's insurance exchanges.[5] Another survey found that 64 percent of respondents had no understanding of the state-based insurance exchanges at the heart of Obamacare.[6]

CNBC conducted an especially revealing survey in 2013, asking half of the respondents if they supported "Obamacare" and the other half if they supported the "Affordable Care Act"—two names for the same law. Thirty percent of respondents didn't know what the Affordable Care Act was, while only 12 percent didn't know "Obamacare."[7] The poll went on to find:

> 29 percent of the public supports Obamacare compared with 22 percent who support ACA. Forty-six percent oppose Obamacare and 37 percent oppose ACA. So putting Obama in the name raises the positives and the negatives. Gender and partisanship are responsible for the differences. Men, independents and Republicans are more negative on Obamacare than ACA. Young people, Democrats, nonwhites and women are more positive on Obamacare.

None of this should come as a surprise. Medicaid (the federal program to pay for medical care for the poor) and Medicare (federal health insurance for the elderly) have been around for almost half a century, and they're constantly in the news, yet around 40 percent of Americans don't know the difference between the two programs.[8]

How can there be such overwhelming ignorance about the issue that Obama put at the heart of his agenda as president? It's less surprising when you realize that many Americans don't even understand the basics of their own health insurance. "It is strange, in my opinion, that the insurance market has evolved so, that so few individuals understand the fundamentals of the medical insurance plans they are insured under," remarked Professor George Loewenstein of Carnegie Mellon University. He led a study, published in September 2013, that found that only 14 percent of Americans understand the basic insurance concepts of "deductible, copay, co-insurance and out-of-pocket maximum."[9] Another study found that people don't even know what they think they know. All of the participants believed that they knew what "co-pay" signified, while only 72 percent actually understood the term. Only 11 percent of people in the study could figure out what a hypothetical, but simple, insurance plan would do for them on a four-day hospital stay.[10]

How about energy policy? Once again, most people are staggeringly ignorant about an issue that affects everyone in one way or another. The 2013 University of Texas at Austin Energy Poll found that the American public knows very little about policies that are politically consequential. After years of populist rhetoric about "energy independence" from one president after another and a decade of alarms about our consumption of Middle Eastern oil, voters are completely confused. Pollsters asked, "*Which country do you believe is the largest foreign supplier of oil for the U.S.?*" Fifty-eight percent of the respondents said Saudi Arabia. Only 13 percent gave the correct answer, which is Canada. The poll found that 82 percent of Americans think the federal government should focus on developing more natural gas, yet only 38 percent of those who had heard of hydraulic fracturing ("fracking"), the most efficient way to extract natural gas, support its use.[11]

Education policy? The Common Core Curriculum—our national education reform du jour—details what K–12 students should know in English and math at the end of each grade. Supported by the Obama administration, the Common Core is touted as a comprehensive education reform for the entire nation (except for a few recalcitrant states). Yet a PDK/Gallup poll finds that 62 percent of

Americans have never even heard of Common Core.[12] Only 45 percent of parents with children in public schools have ever heard of the initiative.[13]

Sometimes wide public ignorance is not merely discouraging but dangerous. Since the beginning of this century, many of the most consequential decisions facing our country's leaders have been concerned with the Middle East. Yet five years after September 11, 2001—despite the inundation of media coverage of the region—63 percent of twenty-somethings, who grew up with America at war in Iraq, couldn't locate that country on a map of the Middle East.[14] Seventy percent could not find Iran (the topic of much conversation these days) or Israel (one of the our closest allies for more than fifty years, not to mention the birthplace of two of the world's great religions). Ninety percent couldn't find Afghanistan on a map of Asia. Seventy-five percent of those polled couldn't find Indonesia—Barack Obama's boyhood home and the site of one of the greatest natural disasters in modern history, the tsunami of 2004. A large majority didn't know that Indonesia was a Muslim nation—the world's most populous Muslim-majority nation, actually. And 54 percent were unaware that there was a country called "Sudan."

Such ignorance is not confined to one party. During preparations for the Iraq War and more recently in the debate over the response to Iran's nuclear program, advocates on both sides used polling numbers to buttress their positions. But how can we trust a consensus about war and peace when the public lacks a basic understanding of what goes on in those lands thousands of miles away?

Most proponents and opponents of all-encompassing healthcare policy, fracking, or the Common Core—whatever they may actually know about these issues—have ideological reasons for their positions. More Americans than we'd like to think rationalize their views out of partisanship, which they think is a shortcut to knowledge. There is too much at stake to worry about specifics, because winning a consequential political battle means the ability to win on other fronts, not only the one you're engaged in at the moment.

The perfect example of this unhealthy democratic aversion to independence of thought is the reaction to the National Security Agency's surveillance programs. Voters' views on the issue flipped under the Bush and Obama administrations. A June 2013 Pew Research Center poll found that 56 percent of voters think that tracking millions of American phone records is "acceptable"; 64 percent of Democrats approve, while only 52 percent of Republicans do. In 2006, when Bush was running the show, a similar poll asked about the government's listening "in on phone calls and reading emails without court approval." Back then, 75 percent of Republicans found such practices "acceptable," while a mere 36 percent of Democrats did.[15]

Most voters cannot understand the minutiae of fiscal reform. Indeed, most investors don't even understand how their own portfolios work. A poll by the brokerage firm Edward Jones in the summer of 2013 found that a third of investors between the ages of eighteen and thirty-four had "no idea" how interest rates affect a portfolio. Even among investors aged sixty-five and older, a quarter had "no idea."[16] (When interest rates rise, the price, or value, of bonds will decrease.)

There are similarly alarming levels of confusion about inflation. When *Business Insider* asked five hundred respondents to state the current inflation rate, about 30 percent came within a percentage point of the correct answer. About 40 percent said the inflation rate was at least 5 percent, and 22 percent believed it was in double digits. On average, respondents said inflation was at 32 percent. The actual rate of inflation at the time of the poll was 1.5 percent, below the Federal Reserve's target of 2 percent and below the historical average.[17]

Few things trigger fear and misconception more than economic tribulation, and nothing prompts elected officials to react with more simplistic populism. The financial crisis of 2007–2008 terrified Americans, and politicians, riding that wave of fear, crammed through all kinds of pet legislation, much of it terribly wrongheaded. How many of us are aware that those "derivatives" politicians railed against allow investors and companies to hedge bets and take insurance on risk? The Mars candy company, for example, likes to dip into the derivatives market to insulate itself from fluctuations in the price of sugar and chocolate. But politicians would lead you to believe that Beelzebub himself had invented these financial tools. With voters in a froth, Congress produced the Dodd-Frank Wall Street Reform and Consumer Protection Act, one of the most complicated pieces of legislation in history. This gargantuan financial regulatory act affects everyone in the marketplace and forever changes the dynamics of the financial sector. Dodd-Frank immediately generated 13,789 pages of new rules. How many Americans could intelligently discuss any aspect of this law?

Voters were satisfied that something had been done about the Wall Street shenanigans that nearly sent all of us to the poor house. But how many are aware that Dodd-Frank includes a payback to unions in the form of a "proxy access" that allows them to manipulate corporate boards? How many are aware that the bill may give the Treasury Department the right to seize private property and businesses without meaningful judicial review? How many know about the so-called "consumer protection board" that slathers more needless regulations on a wide range of businesses? How many voters know that the law inhibits "angel investors"—wealthy individuals who invest in startups with few regulatory guidelines? From Google to Facebook, it was angel investors who undertook the initial risk. What is appropriate risk? Should the democratic process decide? It does. Democracy has snatched this judgment call from investors and entrepreneurs and handed it over to politicians and bureaucrats, who have every incentive to avoid risk.

It is easy to fall into the trap of believing that democracy will improve the function of policy. Lots of people, reasonably dismayed by the last several years of Federal Reserve policy, want more democratic oversight. I once believed in that myself on the grounds that monetary policy should be "transparent." The problem is that many people, including me, tend to confuse transparency with politicizing—that is to say, democratizing. Imagine hundreds of politicians, egged on by 50 million people who have no idea what "quantitative easing" means, running the Fed instead of a board that is largely immune from the forces of populist management.[18] "In God we trust," we proclaim on the back of every dollar bill. But until God decides to communicate his preferred policy with the clarity he demonstrated on Mount Sinai, we might do best to trust the experts, even with their undeniable flaws.

CHAPTER 4

HERD MENTALITY

There are known knowns; there are things we know we know.
We also know there are known unknowns; that is to say we know
there are some things we do not know.
But there are also unknown unknowns—the ones we don't know we
don't know.
—Donald Rumsfeld[1]

As for me, all I know is that I know nothing.
—Socrates

Many Americans view political rallies as inspiring manifestations of our democratic tradition. Thousands of everyday folks who value civic engagement find the time to get involved in the political process, put on funny hats, and cheer for their standard bearer. I, on the other hand, see nothing but sycophantic mobs who have lost their senses. Partisan politics is an organic and unavoidable part of human affairs, but that doesn't make it healthy. If individual voters are irrational, irresponsible, and uneducated, I can only imagine how those faults are exacerbated when they join a crowd.

In 1895, the French social psychologist and sociologist Gustave Le Bon, the "father of crowd psychology," wrote his best-known work, *The Crowd: A Study of the Popular Mind*. Focusing on the collective actions of juries, assemblies, political movements, and religious sects in the changing world of the late nineteenth century, Le Bon concluded that crowds "never thirsted after truth.... Whoever can supply them with illusions is easily their master; whoever attempts to destroy their illusions is always their victim."

Le Bon conceded that crowds are sporadically capable of engaging in good works, but they are usually unreasonable, immoral, and destructive. Individuals in crowds, he observed, blunt their intellectual awareness to conform. Crowds, after all, tend to speak in one voice. Even if your opinions are distinct from the others', once you join the crowd you are more likely to submit to its view than to win it over to yours. Large groups, then, rarely venture from their initial beliefs. Not that most people who join crowds are intellectually curious to begin with. A person in a group tends to stop thinking independently, if he ever did, and becomes instead an "automaton who has ceased to be guided by will," a pawn for a larger cause. As more automatons join the movement, the one-time individual becomes confident that this vague idea is sacred truth. The crowd thus per-petuates itself, attracting more members. It is true, Le Bon conceded, that the crowd often swarms around what was once a sturdy philo-sophical position, but only after it has been dumbed down, pruned, and distorted beyond recognition. Most individuals can't understand a well-developed philosophical argument anyway, let alone people in a crowd. Individuals join crowds because of a vague understanding of the original idea. Crowds accept the superficiality of their ideas because it is a prerequisite to conforming, which, quite often, is their real goal. And because crowds are incapable of fully understanding complex ideas, leaders explain these ideas to them, and automatons start acting like adherents of cults:

> By many [the leaders] are considered as natural forces, as supernatural powers. They evoke grandiose and vague images in men's minds, but this very vagueness that wraps them in obscurity augments their mysterious power. They are the mysterious divinities hidden behind the tabernacle and the devout only approach in fear and trembling.

How many people, asks Le Bon, have died for causes that they barely understood? Today we might ask how many millions vote for ideas they don't understand? We all feel the pull of being part of something bigger than ourselves.

Some social scientists think that Le Bon's analysis of crowds is too simplistic,[2] but his philosophical and empirical study of crowds has stood up remarkably well to modern criticism. In the 1950s, the psychologist Solomon Asch demonstrated with a series of experi-ments the power of conformity on individuals. He told his subjects that they were participating with a group in a vision test, but the other apparent participants had been instructed how to answer. Asch's collaborators began by answering questions correctly, but then they progressively answered incorrectly. Almost 75 percent of the subjects went along with the false answers at least one time. When asked to write down their answers privately, the subjects correctly answered 98 percent of the time. When all the tests were tallied, Asch averaged out all the findings and found that participants offered the wrong answer approximately one-third of the time.

The spreading of beliefs in spite of underlying evidence is called the "bandwagon effect." We don't know with certainty how strong it is in politics, but the evidence suggests that it is overwhelming. You might expect the bandwagon effect to be strong among partisans, but it is probably more widespread among so-called independents, the people who supposedly think for themselves but are actually less informed, less interested, and more easily swept away with the crowd.[3]

In the early 1950s, a group of researchers incuding Paul Lazarsfeld, one of the most important sociologists of the twentieth century, contended that the electorate was "relatively invulnerable to direct argumentation" and "characterized more by faith than by conviction and by wishful expectation rather than careful prediction of consequences."[4] More recently, Brendan Nyhan and Jason Reifler have studied why people are prone to believe political misinformation, finding that both Republicans and Democrats believe what they do because it's convenient. For example, though the president can do little about the price of a fungible commodity like oil, both Republicans and Democrats are willing, by large margins, to blame a president of the opposite party for high gas prices. They find a similar dynamic on an array of issues. Partisans reject facts not because they have a bias against facts, Nyhan and Reifler argue, but because it's too painful to reject their pre-existing views.

We human beings have a psychological need to conform and live within the template offered us by a larger group. We need, as the political cliché goes, to believe in "things bigger than ourselves," to feel like we are part of movements that matter. We all do this in various ways, whether they are cultural, political, or religious groups. The problem for democracy is that once you join a group, like any other partisan, you will often make rationalizations and justifications for your group no matter its shortcomings. This is a condition of membership. Criticizing your own party is bad for business. Breaches of unity often draw swift retaliation and public shaming. Ronald Reagan had his "Eleventh Commandment": "Thou shalt not speak ill of a fellow Republican." And the Obama years have provided ample confirmation of the rule. When a few liberal pundits conceded that the catastrophic rollout of Obamacare in late 2013 could have gone better, they were attacked for hurting the larger cause. Joan Walsh of Salon.com, one of President Obama's most dutiful public defenders, warned that when "liberals rush conscientiously" to be critical of their own party, even if the criticism is justified, "they only encourage the completely unbalanced and unhinged coverage of whatever the problem may be."[5]

People like Joan Walsh aren't deceiving the public as much as they are deceiving themselves. This is characteristic of being in a crowd: what looks like blind faith and partisanship to others feels like the truth. According to a recent study published in the journal of the Association for Psychological Science, conformity feels like fact.[6] "Conformity gets a bad rap," one of the researchers remarked. "That is partially predicated on the idea that it is a form of lying: you're lying about yourself to try to fit in. Our data suggest that at a deep emotional level you really are changing your view."

Once you have adopted the belief of your group, your confidence in the superiority of that belief is unchallengeable. A study by Kaitlin Toner, a psychology graduate student at Duke University, measured Americans' attitudes on nine contentious political issues to see who felt more superiority about their beliefs and why.[7] Toner found, not surprisingly, that people at the extremes of the political spectrum—both right and left—felt more superior about their views than moderates. Partisanship is an intellectual shortcut. It offers us a template to which we can conform, but it doesn't give us much room to ponder.

Just as irrational as believing your own group is above criticism is believing the other group is always wrong. Lilliana Mason analyzed results from the American National Election Studies from 1972 to 2004, along with other studies that measured voter views: "I asked people questions like, 'When you talk about Democrats (or Republicans), do you say "we" rather than "they"?' When someone insults Democrats, do you feel insulted? I wanted to get a sense of group membership—the extent to which your party identification feels like being part of a team." Mason found that what she calls "behavioral polarization"—strongly biased views and anger at the other side—was rampant among members of both parties. As Mason explains it, they based their positions on "team spirit" rather than strong opinions on public policy.[8]

Mason's findings show how human beings distort their political decision making. Of course, we distort our decision making in lots of other areas as well. *Psychology Today* compiled a list of fifty common cognitive distortions.[9] Reading through the list, you begin to realize these distortions are not only common in politics but foundational to democracy. Here are some of the most common:

Negative Predictions: "Overestimating the likelihood that an action will have a negative outcome." For example, insisting that failure to pass climate-change legislation today means that you will be scuba diving to see the Empire State Building within a few years. Democracy gives politicians the incentive to predict the worst if voters reject them.

Catastrophizing: "Thinking of unpleasant events as catastrophes." Harry Truman supposedly said that when your neighbor loses his job it's a recession, but when you lose your jobs it's a depression. Every election is the most consequential in history—just as the last one was. Politics is the art of sensationalizing our current predicaments. Liberal politicians, for example, can't go on television without declaring that we have just been through the worst economic calamity since the Great Depression (a highly arguable contention). How often do we hear that "Washington is more polarized than ever before" as we face "unprecedented" gridlock? When the voter is faced with such a daunting environment, he is not in a position to make rational decisions about candidates or policy. In *The Myth of the Rational Voter*, the economist Bryan Caplan calls this "pessimistic bias." One of the most prevalent drivers of irrationality in voters is a "tendency to overestimate the severity of economic problems and underestimate the (recent) past, present, and future performance of the economy."

All-or-Nothing Thinking: Example: If we do not adopt a specific Democratic/Republican economic policy, we will suffer irreparable harm.

Delusions: "Holding a fixed, false belief despite overwhelming evidence to the contrary." We have already reviewed many of these beliefs, but there is no end to voters' delusions about the power of politicians to change things.

The Halo Effect: "For example, perceiving high-calorie foods as lower in calories if they're accompanied by a salad." An example from politics is politicians' referring to a slowing of the growth of government spending as a "cut." The halo effect allows politicians to claim credit for achievements that are ephemeral or trivial.

Failure to Consider Alternative Explanations: "Coming up with one explanation for…something…and failing to consider alternative, more likely explanations." This cognitive distortion was on display after the economic crisis of 2008. Republicans blamed government, cronyism, and imprudent regulation. Democrats blamed free markets, unfettered capitalism, and lack of regulation. Neither side could entertain the possibility of a combination of these causes.

The Self-Serving Bias: "[P]eople's tendency to attribute positive events to their own character but attribute negative events to external factors." This bias is, of course, the primary job of any political campaign.

Overgeneralizing: "Generalizing a belief that may have validity in some situations (such as 'If you want something done well, you should do it yourself.') to every situation."

Biased Implicit Attitudes: Subconsciously associating one thing with another, for example, "fat" with "lazy." This distortion is one of the main drivers of political debate. Democrats try to associate Republicans with wealthy white plutocrats, while Republicans try to associate Democrats with effete latte sippers.

The Tendency to Prefer Familiar Things: We like what's familiar. Studies have shown that among the most important determinants of political identification are your parents, your friends, and where you live.

Equally prevalent in our democratic discourse are logical fallacies. It is difficult to find a political speech that doesn't commit at least one. At the root of direct democracy, in fact, is the fallacy of the false dilemma, the insistence that there are only two possible choices in a given situation. There are many other fallacies at work in our politics. Here are some of the most common.[10]

The Slippery Slope: A conclusion based on the premise that if A happens, then B through Z must eventually happen. To avoid Z, therefore, we must avoid A. For example, if we restrict late-term abortions, then before long women will again find themselves in back alleys.

Post Hoc Ergo Propter Hoc: If B occurs after A, then A must have caused B. So if the president gives a speech about the economy on Thursday, and on Friday the jobs report is terrible, then the president's speeches are killing the economy. The electorate is highly susceptible to linking causation to chronology.

Genetic Fallacy: This is the argument that the origins of a person, an organization, or an idea determine its character, nature, or worth. So any anti-poverty plan proposed by a Republican is a bad idea because Republicans don't care about the poor.

Begging the Claim: The conclusion that the writer should prove is validated within the claim. For example: "Diversity is our strength" or "The only solution to democracy's problem is more democracy."

Ad Hominem: This is an attack on the character of the person making an argument instead of a response to the argument. For an example, I refer you to every political campaign in the history of mankind.

Ad Populum: This is an emotional appeal to positive or negative concepts that have no bearing on the validity of your argument. An example is the appeal to patriotism and public safety to justify government's snooping on citizens.

Red Herring: This is a diversionary tactic that avoids the key issues, often by avoiding opposing arguments rather than addressing them. Example: My opponent's tax plan? Did you know he has an offshore account in the Cayman Islands!

Straw Man: This is the fallacy of attacking a distorted version of your opponent's argument rather than responding to his actual argument. President Obama is one of the most creative practitioners of this fallacy. "I reject," he once declared, "the view that … government has no role in laying the foundation for our common prosperity."[11] So does everyone else except a handful of anarchists. Straw men populate most of the president's arguments.

Moral Equivalence: There has to be room for hyperbole in political talk, but it is common to draw a comparison between misdeeds of quite incomparable gravity. In America, there seems to be an irresistible temptation to compare your opponent to Hitler. In late 2013, when the bottom seemed to be falling out of the Obama administration, the White House advisor John Podesta confirmed his ferociously partisan reputation by declaring that the president was "facing a second term against a cult worthy of Jonestown in charge of one of the houses of Congress." A comparison of the majority party of the House of Representatives to a cult that slaughtered nine hundred men, women, and children perhaps betrays Podesta's true estimation of the role of reason in our democracy.

Even though politics is drenched in this type of shoddy and lazy thinking, we still tend to think we're independent thinkers. It's difficult, however, to know what we actually think. Beyond sampling biases or phraseology biases, many recent polls prove that Americans will tell pollsters what they think they think, but not how they intend to act. Part of the problem is social desirability bias—people's tendency to give answers that they believe will be viewed favorably by others. There is also confirmation bias—the tendency of people to say things that confirm their beliefs or theories. Whatever the case, voters are fooling themselves in various ways. We are far more partisan than we believe.

For instance, everyone claims to hate politicians. Not long ago, 60 percent of Americans in an NBC News/*Wall Street Journal* poll said that if they could replace every single member of Congress, *including their own representative*, they would do it. This is, of course, untrue. Everyone hates everyone else's congressman. The incumbency business is as good as ever and getting better. After 2012, the Bloomberg Government Barometer found that though approval of Congress was then at an all-time low, nine out of ten members of the House and Senate who ran for reelection were successful.[12] In the Senate, the only loser was Scott Brown of Massachusetts—a Republican who had been elected in unusual circumstances in a deeply blue state. That was an improvement over the 85 percent incumbent success rate of 2010, which was considered a sweeping "change." Perhaps it's not unhealthy that so many people feel so well represented, but these numbers don't suggest a populace pining to get rid of their representatives. Democracy is easy on incumbents.

Americans also claim to desire more choices. Do they really? A Gallup poll finds that 60 percent of Americans believe that the major political parties have done such an appalling job representing their constituents that the system is in dire need of a third party. A meager 26 percent believe that the two major parties are adequately representing America. That's the lowest approval rating for the two established parties in the ten years that Gallup has asked the question.[13] The thing is, we already have a third party—and a fourth, a fifth, and a sixth—and very few people give them even the slightest consideration. Despite what they tell pollsters, most voters are not willing to waste their vote on a third-party candidate. Throwing inconsequential moral support behind a third party makes people feel virtuous (even though, in the end, it would mean less representation for those voters, not more). We know this because of an extensive two-hundred-year test case.

We value partisanship over issues that we explicitly claim to care about. Polls reliably find, for instance, that the national debt is one of the primary concerns of the average American voter, who still claims to believe in small and responsible government. When given an array of choices—education, national security, environment, etc.—and asked to prioritize them, respondents almost always place national debt as one of their top issues. How worried could they really be, though? When was the last time a politician won an election with a plan that spent less and cut more? When was the last time a majority of Americans supported reforms that would deal with the deficit in any meaningful way? Broadly speaking, voters want to tackle the debt problem. But they don't like any of the specifics. Poll after poll finds that a majority of voters believe cutting America's debt is vital, but hardly any of them support realistic measures to accomplish it. Every attempt to reform any part of the entitlement system is met with an outcry from voters. Americans are willing to cut military spending and tax the rich. We could have an army the size of the Belizean marines and set the tax rate at 100 percent for everyone with an income of over a million dollars, and it wouldn't make a dent in the long-term debt. So either Americans don't get what the debt problem really looks like or they don't really care. Maybe they hear so much about it that they think they should worry (and they should). Or maybe the debt in their lives has serious consequences, so they feel compelled to say they're apprehensive. Americans, though, have never really felt the consequences of government debt. So we may say we care, but we sure don't vote like we do.

Since 2005, according to Gallup, at least half of Americans have been saying the government has too much power, and by 2013 six in ten Americans supposedly held that opinion.[14] But other than words, how have they demonstrated their belief that government has grown too big? Americans have elected two presidents who have vastly expanded the scope of government, and both of them won reelection rather comfortably. Major initiatives have expanded government into education, healthcare, financial markets, and surveillance, to name just a few areas. President Obama won his office rather convincingly twice, and whatever you make of his policies, he's consistently preached about the moral imperative of expanding the reach of government's hand. Left-wing populism is more successful than ever, and the Democrats' consolidation of partisan power under Obama is one of the most successful in years. So when you bore down into the numbers there are few places Americans are willing to cut back power or shake off partisanship. It's more likely that voters view government as having too much power when government is being run by someone else.

Much of the electorate lacks either the interest or the capacity (through their own fault or the fault of our educational system) to become educated on the most rudimentary level. Most of us operate politically on a terribly superficial level; we don't understand what our votes are actually doing. Some of this ignorance is rational—the cost of deeply educating ourselves on policy would be greater than the benefit. Some of it reflects a lack of interest or laziness. And some of it comes from the cognitive distortions that feed on groupthink. Politics—even if we try our best to stay current and discern the truth—is infused with incentives that bring out the worst in groups of voters.

PART II

THE IDEA

For You O Democracy

Come, I will make the continent indissoluble,
I will make the most splendid race the sun ever shone upon,
I will make divine magnetic lands,
With the love of comrades,
With the life-long love of comrades.

I will plant companionship thick as trees along all the rivers of America,
and along the shores of the great lakes, and all over the prairies,
I will make inseparable cities with their arms about each other's necks,
By the love of comrades,
By the manly love of comrades.

For you these from me, O Democracy, to serve you ma femme!
For you, for you I am trilling these songs.
—WALT WHITMAN

CHAPTER 5

PHILOSOPHER KINGS

Authority has always attracted the lowest elements in the human race. All through history mankind has been bullied by scum. Those who lord it over their fellows and toss commands in every direction and would boss the grass in the meadow about which way to bend in the wind are the most depraved kind of prostitutes. They will submit to any indignity, perform any vile act, do anything to achieve power. The worst off-sloughings of the planet are the ingredients of sovereignty. Every government is a parliament of whores. The trouble is, in a democracy the whores are us.
—P. J. O'Rourke, *Parliament of Whores*

Whither haste ye, O men? Yea, verily ye know not that ye are doing none of the things ye ought ...
—Plato, *Cleitophon*

Understanding the fallibility of human nature is only the first step in understanding the problems inherent in democracy. How we balance individual freedom, a healthy state, security, and our religious beliefs is a topic that has been on the minds of thinkers since ancient times. The two most prominent classical critics of democracy, Plato and Aristotle, also happen to be two of the greatest philosophers in history. Plato offered a counter-ideal: a utopian republic. Aristotle compared political systems and found the best in the mean, in a mixed constitutional government.

Plato, it can be argued, was a liberal technocrat, a benevolent fascist, and a theocratic conservative all rolled into one deeply unpleasant human being. Plato supported a "tyranny of reason" over the dynamism of individual liberty, yes, but we shouldn't reject him too hastily. Some of his political thinking was undoubtedly driven by democratic Athens sentencing his teacher and friend Socrates to death—a perfect example of how democracy and freedom are not necessarily compatible. Socrates, a nuisance to the corrupt, even if democratic, Athenian state, was found guilty of "impiety" for challenging the city's gods and of perverting the innocent minds of young people. As a good Athenian, Socrates staunchly defended democracy even as a jury of his peers—at least five hundred of them, probably many more—convicted him.

In his book *What's Wrong with Democracy?* Loren J. Samons II, a professor of Classical Studies at Boston University, describes the Athenian government:

> Athens's history under *demokratia* shows the Athenian people voting repeatedly to make war on their former friends and allies (as well as enemies), to conclude alliances with their recent enemies or with Greeks that had

collaborated with Persia, to execute or exile their own leaders, to extort monetary payments from allied states that wished to be free of Athenian hegemony, to use this extorted money to fund Athenian projects (including the extortion of more money), to impose their own form of government on formerly autonomous states by force, to execute and enslave thousands of non-Athenian Greeks … to require religious oaths and loyalty from allies … and to grant honors to the very dynasts who imperiled their own form of government.[1]

Plato was less enamored of the political system that killed his mentor, though he was no less critical of non-democratic Sparta and of the Athenian oligarchy that was established after Sparta's defeat of Athens in the Peloponnesian War.

Plato puts politics on a higher plane than most political reporters do. He argues that the point of politics is "making preparations for the citizens' souls to be as good as possible." Not surprisingly, given that he thought politics was about encouraging virtuous souls, he had some serious problems with what you and I might refer to as campaign rhetoric—the flattery, the scintillating promises, the scare-mongering, the insipid sloganeering, the attempt to elicit emotional (rather than rational) responses—all the familiar democratic BS (for lack of a better term).

In the dialogue *Gorgias*, Plato writes:

Now what about the rhetoric directed toward the Athenian people and the other peoples of free men in the cities— what in the world is it, in our view? Do the rhetors in your opinion always speak with a view to the best, aiming at this, that because of their speeches the citizens shall be as good as possible? Or do these men too strive for gratifying the citizens and, for the sake of their own private interest, make light of the common interest, and associate with the peoples as if with children, trying only to gratify them, and giving no heed to whether they will be better or worse because of these things?

The problem with this sort of rhetoric—now nearly the sole purpose of political speech—is the degree to which it debases the very people it aims to lift up. It is not, as Plato would point out, interested in truth or in what is truly good. It instead manipulates by dangling before the mob promises of free lunches.

Democratic political rhetoric, perhaps in Plato's time and certainly in our own, condenses to the baser passions of men; dumbing down debates (remember in 2007 when a moderator prompted Republican candidates to raise their hands if they did not believe in evolution); and reducing us to gotcha politics, which is never reasoned politics. Democracy, unfortunately, plays to the crowd and, as campaign consultants know, you can move the crowd with attack ads, even if such ads can spiral downward into intentionally misleading speech.

Plato's entire system of political philosophy turns on the analogy that the governance of a city (by which he means the people in general) is the governance of a person within himself writ large. So that as a man rules himself, then the city rules itself. And the man who can best rule himself is the philosopher fully engaged with the truth. The opinions of the majority are of little significance compared to the reality of truth. Reason, the highest and most noble part of the soul, is what should guide the philosopher and the state. It is reason that makes law and order possible, and the best governor is the man who understands virtue, which is what is "always the same, immortal, and true."

You might not be wholly astonished to find out that the ideal rulers sound a lot like … Plato! Because to Plato, the majority of mankind is in dire need of moral philosophers to point it in the right direction; no shock, when this is your view of the masses:

> … they always look down at the ground like cattle, and, with their heads bent over the dinner table, they feed, fatten, and fornicate. To outdo others in these things, they kick and butt them with iron horns and hooves, killing each other, because their desires are insatiable. For the part that they're trying to fill is like a vessel full of holes, and neither it nor the things they are trying to fill it with are among the things that are.

Now, it is inarguable that we, the people, tend to feed, fatten, and fornicate quite a bit. And it is inarguable that we don't know, well, a lot. But clearly most people want to achieve and accomplish far more than Plato gives them credit for. Still, Plato believes everyone has a role to play in the best form of government. Some are born to work, some are born to fight, and some are born to rule. Plato's Republic is a unity where everything is done, and everyone is accorded his proper task, on the grounds of what is true, what is best, within the dictates of reason. In the lowest class are the artisans and workers who provide for the most basic necessities of the city; next is the lower guardian class tasked with defense and warfare; and then the upper guardian class, which governs the city. Within this utopia, the upper guardians' wives, children, property, and meals are held in common; no child knows his parents, no parent his child, universal pre-K is the rule—no child is left behind!—all in an effort to cement unity. Because most people are incapable of reasoning their way to a virtuous life, the city is governed by a philosopher-king who can lead the way.

Plato believed that democratic man is irresponsible, unreliable, ill-mannered, and materialistic. Because democracy does not teach men how to order their lives or control their desires, it descends to licentiousness and chaos, to disordered and insatiable passions, to men enslaved by their own lusts, which makes them easy prey for the tyrant. Democracy is the gateway to tyranny, because men who cannot control themselves must be controlled by others. Plato's Republic aims to avoid such tyranny with authoritarian rule that protects the people from themselves, that offers men freedom from disorder—but not freedom as you and I might recognize it.

Aristotle, in this sense, is more modern, not to mention more moderate. He argues that the best government is a mixed government. He distinguishes between six forms of government, three true and three perversions. Monarchy, aristocracy, and constitutional rule (polity) are marked as good forms of government; tyranny, oligarchy, and democracy are their respective distortions, which aim not for the common good, but to serve private, selfish interests or the interests of a particular class or group.

Aristotle believes that the state is a natural outgrowth of man's being a political animal who lives in society. Contrary to Plato, who subordinates the family to the state, for Aristotle the family is the seedbed or the building block of the state; it is where one learns the political and social virtues. As with the family, Aristotle believes "a state exists for the sake of a good life, and not for the sake of life only."

As with Plato, the good life is to be found in the practice of reason and virtue, and promoting virtue is a proper role of the state:

> Whereas, those who care for good government take into consideration virtue and vice in states. Whence it may be further inferred that virtue must be the care of a state which is truly so called, and not merely enjoys the name: for without this end the community becomes a mere alliance which differs only in place from alliances of which the members live apart; and law is only a convention ... and has no real power to make the citizens good and just.

The problem with democracy, in Aristotle's scheme, is that it gives power to demagogues who do not rule for the common good and who have no interest in promoting virtue. Instead, they promote "equality," pitting the poor against the rich, and a false form of freedom, which is really licentiousness and lawlessness. The tool of tyrants is the power of the democratic mob.

Conversely, Aristotle argues, the good form of majority rule—polity—is the right ordering of consensus in harmony with virtue and law. To do this, the constitutional polity incorporates elements of monarchical, aristocratic, and democratic rule (sort of the way the Founding Fathers did with the president, the Senate, and the House of Representatives). The virtuous man follows the golden mean—the right centering of virtue between the extremes of where virtue turns to vice—and so does a well-ordered polity.

A great defender of this political golden mean is the moderation of the middle classes who are "least likely to shrink from rule, or to be over-ambitious for it," and least likely to see politics as mere jostling for the "political supremacy" that looks "only to the interest of their own form of government": oligarchy for the rich, egalitarian democracy for the poor. A large middle class, in contrast, is best suited to support a constitutional government of laws that supports the common good.

Aristotle, being less utopian and more willing to consider experience and circumstances than Plato, refrains from giving too many specifics about his perfect government. Each state must determine based on many factors—from geography to demography to wealth—the constitution that can best achieve the goal of virtue and good government. Virtue was central to Plato and Aristotle, that only virtuous men could make a virtuous state and so therefore the state had an interest in promoting virtue. You don't hear much about that today. But we do see and hear quite a lot of politicians promising anything to get elected, pitting groups against groups, and doling out taxpayer-funded freebies from the federal government.

The lack of virtue, as Plato and Aristotle would have understood it, points up a lack of something else: stability. Stability—reliable laws, strong social structures (primarily the family and community), the free operation of social institutions unhindered by an interventionist state—is essential to a healthy society and yet is undermined by the wayward, revolutionary currents of democracy, which presses for "change" (a word loved by politicians but that has no tangible moral or policy value), radical individualism, and radical egalitarianism, all of which are inherent in classical democracy. However flawed Plato's solution, he and Aristotle at least identified a big part of democracy's problem. Their classical critique is a necessary corrective to our usually unreflective, unthinking praise of "democracy," which in their view was neither the freest nor the best form of government. It was, in fact, a perversion.

Living a good moral life is important to individual fulfillment. The idea that government can induce us to a moral life—though we can certainly quibble with a definition of "moral"—is a popular notion today. As Kenneth Minogue once put it:

> Life is a better teacher of virtue than politicians, and most sensible governments in the past left moral faults alone. Instead, democratic citizenship in the twenty first century means receiving a stream of "messages" from authority. Some may forgive these intrusions because they are well intentioned. Who would defend prejudice, debt, or excessive drinking? The point, however, is that rulers have no business telling us how to live. They are tiresome enough in their exercise of authority. They are intolerable when they mount the pulpit. We should never doubt that nationalizing the moral life is the first step in totalitarianism.

Today, in this country, we nationalize through democratic means.

For our purposes, one of the distinguishing and vital aspects of a healthy liberal state is the protection of the rights of minorities. Ancient thinkers were concerned with this problem, none more so than the rhetorician, philosopher, and theologian St. Augustine (354–430), bishop of Hippo in North Africa, who lived at a time of great upheaval within the Roman Empire. After a wild youth, Augustine converted to the Catholic faith and devoted much of his intellectual energy to the theological controversies of his day. The greatest crisis, however, that Augustine faced was the common belief that the abandonment of the pagan gods was responsible for the sack of Rome in 410 and the instability of the empire. The rise of anti-Christian feeling led Augustine to write one of his greatest books, *The City of God*.

One of the most important works in Western civilization, this historical, theological, and philosophical study of the "two cities"—the City of God and the City of Man—explores the place of Christians in a pagan world. It could be said that Augustine's entire political project is the reconciliation of the Christian religion with the temporal authority of Rome. Citizens of the City of God, he argued, are also citizens of the City of Man, and their dual allegiance is no threat to the state.

In the United States, with its extraordinarily diverse population, multiple allegiances are taken for granted. A man doesn't have to conform to the majority in religion or practically any other matter of belief, affection, or taste. He maintains an allegiance to his hometown, his family and ethnic group, his school, his profession, his church, his political party, and of course his country. The latter is not, as some statists would insist, a commitment to the reigning consensus or party line but to the liberal ideals that make the system we live under possible.

From a historical perspective, it is nothing short of a miracle that so many people from so many backgrounds—often with long histories of bloody conflict with one another—get along and even thrive in this country. Protestants and Catholics, Pakistanis and Indians, can live in the same country, sometimes the same neighborhood, without killing each other. The miracle of diversity goes beyond ancient tribal identities, however. A man can live in peace the life of a secular gay urbanite in San Francisco or an evangelical outdoorsman in Colorado Springs, finding others who share his values and tastes. We can enjoy this diversity in part because of our geography—we have the luxury in this huge country of spreading out—but America's Constitution is also crucial. Democracy impinges only slightly on our individual choices because government is limited. Even when democracy does affect your choices, the effect traditionally has been localized and divided—different strokes for different folks. This gives us tremendous space. The democratization and centralization of these decisions undermine this diversity. Every American is in some sense a Christian in Rome. But as democracy homogenizes government from coast to coast, we'll all be offering the same sacrifice to the emperor.

Considering the forms of government in the City of Man, Augustine follows the judgment of Plato and Aristotle about the good forms (monarchy, aristocracy, and polity) and the perversions of those forms (tyranny, oligarchy, and democracy). Unlike his pagan predecessors, however, Augustine counsels Christians to accept with humility the government under which providence has placed them, regardless of that government's success in achieving its ends. He doesn't oppose the reform of government, but he insists that Christians are called at all times to practice virtue, seeking to expand the unseen City of God, however unpropitious the circumstances.

For Augustine, the chief concern of earthly government is justice. The word appears on nearly every page of *The City of God*, and it figures prominently in Augustine's discussion of the Roman Republic, which bears on the topic of democracy. Among the handful of Americans who give any thought to the origins of our Constitution, many assume that its principles were derived from republican Rome. But unlike twenty-first-century Americans, citizens of the Roman Republic cared most about justice, not equality.

In a prescient passage in *The City of God*, Augustine quotes a passage from Cicero's dialogue *De re publica* in which Scipio, using a musical analogy that was common in ancient and medieval political philosophy, describes the proper ordering of a commonwealth—that is, a state that serves the common good:

> [S]o where reason is allowed to modulate the diverse elements of the state, there is obtained a perfect concord from

the upper, lower, and middle classes as from various
sounds; and what musicians call harmony in singing, is
concord in matters of state, which is the strictest bond and
best security of any republic....[2]

All classes of men are bound together harmoniously in this classical
commonwealth, not seeking sameness or equality, but the common
good. And the state thus organized must be governed in "the most
absolute justice." This just governance may be "by a monarch, or an
aristocracy, or by the whole people."

Whenever any of these forms of government—even the rule of
the people—rules unjustly, it is transformed into a tyranny. Relying
on Cicero, Augustine warns that when the "people themselves are
unjust, and become … themselves the tyrant, then the republic is not
only blemished … it altogether ceases to be." A populace reduced to
this sorry condition ceases to be a "people" in the political sense. It
delights in the "scandalous iniquities" of the pagan gods, applauding
"not those who protect their interests, but those who provide them
with pleasure."[3] Augustine's description of this degraded state fits,
with striking precision, our modern democratic society. The people
desire their state to "remain undefeated, … flourish[ing] and
abound[ing] in resources, … secure in peace, … every man … able
to increase his wealth." He continues,

Let no severe duty be commanded, no impurity forbid-
den…. Let the laws take cognizance rather of the injury
done to one's own person. If a man be a nuisance to his
neighbor, or injure his property, family, or person, let him
be actionable; but in his own affairs let every one with
impunity do what he will in company with his own family,

and with those who willingly join him…. If such happiness is distasteful to any, let him be branded as a public enemy; and if any attempt to modify or put an end to it, let him be silenced, banished, put an end to.[4]

This disordered state is purely instrumental to individuals' search for pleasure or what seems attractive, instead of what is truly good. God's law is absent from the decisions of the people as a whole, since there is no authentic community. In its place is a rabble seeking to have its passions met by approval from politicians who cravenly appease them.

Out of the shade of Augustine steps the more than monumental figure of St. Thomas Aquinas: a Dominican theologian and philosopher of the High Middle Ages. He was trained in many of the universities throughout Europe at the time and spent most of his years as a teacher and theologian coalescing and harmonizing the seemingly disparate elements of the natural philosophical system of Aristotle and Scripture. How do religious people live within the secular world?

For our purposes in discussing democracy, though, Thomas makes the same distinctions in forms of government as we have seen from Plato, Aristotle, and Augustine—it's actually a mode of distinguishing that has served as the way of understanding political regimes for more than two thousand years. To refresh, the good forms of state powers are monarchy, aristocracy, and polity; the perversions are tyranny, oligarchy, and democracy, respectively.

Now, when Aristotle argued for these political sorts, he used these distinctions not as precise points on a map but rather areas on a spectrum that oftentimes merged with one another, sometimes serving the common good, at others, serving the interests of factions only. This is to say that there is undoubtedly mixture in political constitutions.

So, just as the human soul and person are to be ruled over by reason—the highest power of the mind—it makes sense, for Thomas, that this order extends to the association of persons in society. As such, we shall take up the discussion of Thomas with order and precise direction.

Analogously, the community of men is in disarray as each one pursues his proper end without all of these activities being guided to a goal that encompasses and surpasses them. This superior purpose is known appropriately as the common good, but it does not abrogate the fittingness and necessity of the more proximate and particular ends of smaller groups and institutions, such as the family, for instance.

While Thomas is quick to remind the reader that each person is instilled with reason that gives him some of the tools necessary to meet his end, man by nature is a social animal, inclined to live in social and political community with other persons. As such, since each person cannot be a king unto himself, cutting himself off from his fellows, there must, by nature, be an element that governs the whole, establishing peace and ordering the group to ends that exceed survival.

This leads to Thomas's taking up the question of whether it is fitting that the state be ruled by "one man or by many." Going back to what we stated regarding reason as the directive principle within the person, Thomas aims to show that this argument holds true also in matters pertaining to political society. Since reason aims to properly order the passions and other aspects of the person in concord with the principles and rule of reason, which is peace, it may rightly be said that reason is the means by which peaceful unity is established in the person as a whole.

After a number of counter-positions raising the supposed point that Scripture does not provide for the adequate establishment of kings and rulers, Thomas states his position: "But the beauty of the institutions of a people depends on the right institution of its rulers."[5] Since, therefore, the beauty of the government of a people is manifested through the beauty of its rulers (beauty here is not to be understood in the cosmetic sense, but rather in terms of the right proportions of law, justice, mercy, and virtue to one another), this leads Thomas to comment on two important aspects on the "right institution of rulers in any political community or people."

The first aspect is that "all citizens should participate in the regime." Such inclusivity is a clear look back to Aristotle's notion of keeping order and peace through having all share in government. In seeking such participation, however, Thomas is not advocating for the supremacy of democracy as the governing political power. The second aspect is that given the beneficial characteristics of all forms of government according to the classical distinction between good types and respective perversions, the best form of political community, practically speaking, is an admixture of monarchy, aristocracy, and rule of the people. As Thomas writes:

> And so the best institution of rulers belongs to a city or kingdom in which one person is chosen by reason of his virtue to rule over all, and other persons govern under him by reason of their virtue. And yet such a regime belongs to all citizens, both because its rulers are chosen from the citizens, and because all citizens choose its rulers. For this

is the best constitution, a happy mixture of kingdom, since one person rules; and of aristocracy, since many govern by reason of their virtue; and of government by the people, since rulers can be chosen from the people, and since the choice of rulers belongs to the people.[6]

As is apparent, Thomas's vision for the best government, while composed within the framework of monarchy, is not an exposition or defense of the enlightened despot, the benevolent dictator, or the absolute monarch. It is tempered with checks and balances of a sort from the aristocracy and the people as a whole—a sharing of power, with a common end in mind. In fact, later in the article, Thomas makes explicit that the "divine institution of kingship did not give to the kings of Israel any right to make tyrannical law." Tyranny, whether of one king or the masses, as it was for Plato, Aristotle, Augustine, and all classical tradition, is likewise a great evil in Thomas's estimation.

CHAPTER 6

FOUNDING MYTHS

In the case of a word like DEMOCRACY, not only is there no agreed definition, but the attempt to make one is resisted from all sides. It is almost universally felt that when we call a country democratic we are praising it: consequently the defenders of every kind of régime claim that it is a democracy, and fear that they might have to stop using the word if it were tied down to any one meaning. Words of this kind are often used in a consciously dishonest way. That is, the person who uses them has his own private definition, but allows his hearer to think he means something quite different.

—George Orwell, "Politics and
the English Language: An Essay" (1947)[1]

"The world is watching us. We are theoretically its last great democracy."
"Jesus. 'The last great democracy.'"
"The foundation of our democracy is based on the citizens' right to vote. It is our duty as Americans to fulfill that responsibility."
—*Recount* (HBO movie about
the 2000 presidential election showdown)

No matter how you slice it, we're not the world's last great democracy—and we weren't even the first great democracy. Americans have a habit of deploying "democracy" as shorthand for all that is pure and good about government—the antonym of "tyranny." Though we can understand that tendency, we must also recall that if the Founding Fathers had wanted to establish a democracy, they might at least have mentioned it—even once—in the Constitution. (Actually, it may surprise many Americans to learn that the Constitution doesn't even guarantee the right to vote.) If democracy were as morally unassailable as many of us believe, the Founding Fathers—men who, with all their limitations, grappled with the practicalities of self-rule more seriously than anyone else in history—would not have regarded the idea as dangerous.

The Framers of the Constitution, who were keen students of history, wanted to guarantee their countrymen a "republican form of government." Concentrated power, they knew, is eventually inimical to liberty. Like Aristotle, they understood that both republics and democracies had their dangers, especially the latter. "Remember," John Adams warned, "democracy never lasts long. It soon wastes, exhausts, and murders itself. There never was a democracy yet that did not commit suicide."[2]

The Founders carefully examined the fates of the republics that had gone before, and what they saw scared them. The obvious precedent was Rome, but they could also look to the more recent Venetian and Dutch republics—both of which were already in decline when Americans were imagining their own future. The Republic of Poland was collapsing before their eyes. Above all, they had before them the example of the English Commonwealth. Forged in civil war by New England's Puritan cousins, it had burned so brightly and failed so quickly. Within eleven years of the execution of Charles I, the English people, weary of republican chaos, restored the monarchy. The Americans who gathered in Philadelphia, knowing that they had to craft their new republic with infinite care, followed the advice of Demosthenes: "There is one safeguard known generally to the wise, which is an advantage and security to all, but especially to democracies as against despots. What is it? Distrust." Confirmation of the ancient orator's skepticism of democracy followed soon when less cautious revolutionaries in France erected a kingless state whose undivided powers were consolidated in Paris. The path of French democracy led directly to the guillotine.

The American Revolution was unlike any other. It was not a populist uprising—there was no "mob." Nowadays we like to portray it as an uprising of the humble "countryfolk"—the modest farmer leaving his plow and grabbing a musket. That's not how it happened. Yes, members of every class fought for independence, but the rebellion was inspired and led by America's *self-made* aristocracy. David Lefer, the author of *The Founding Conservatives: How a Group of Unsung Heroes Saved the American Revolution*, argues that the Founders would be considered a lot more Wall Street than Main Street these days. "They were members of the upper classes—the colonial 1 percent, if you will—who were among the most ardent defenders of American rights. Many fought with distinction against British Redcoats. But they also wanted to preserve as much of the old order as possible. What the founding conservatives feared was that revolution would bring 'the dissolution of every kind of authority,' as James Wilson, a prosperous Philadelphia lawyer and staunch free-market advocate, put it. Their role, as they saw it, was to keep the revolution from spiraling out of control."[3] This is what Russell Kirk had in mind when he wrote that America's was a revolution "not made but prevented."

America was already rich. Very rich. The colonies had experienced tremendous economic growth in the eighty years leading up to the Revolution. According to some estimates, the gross national product of North America multiplied scores of times between 1650 and 1770. A number of historians think the colonists may have had the highest standard of living in the world at the time of the Revolution. The insurrection against the British government was no uprising of the downtrodden. It was the result of the evolving self-assurance of wealthy farmers and landowners—"conservatives" in the purest sense of the idea.

Though it is common to praise the independent spirit of the Founding generation, sometimes you have to wonder what might have happened if a referendum on independence had been held among the colonial population. Would most of them have chosen war against the mother country or voted to continue with the status quo? One man, one vote might have meant no republic. John Ferling is one of many historians who have pointed out that the Revolutionary cause often enjoys little support among the general public:

> But as the colonists discovered how difficult and dangerous military service could be, enthusiasm waned. Many men preferred to remain home, in the safety of what Gen. George Washington described as their "Chimney Corner." Early in the war, Washington wrote that he despaired of "compleating the army by Voluntary Inlistments." Mindful that volunteers had rushed to enlist when hostilities began, Washington predicted that "after the first emotions are over," those who were willing to serve from a belief in the "goodness of the cause" would amount to little more than "a drop in the Ocean." He was correct. As 1776 progressed,

many colonies were compelled to entice soldiers with offers of cash bounties, clothing, blankets and extended furloughs or enlistments shorter than the one-year term of service established by Congress.[4]

We will never know exactly how opinion was divided among the colonists, but various histories of loyalists in America estimate that 20 to 25 percent remained loyal to the English Crown, while 40 to 45 percent supported the rebellion.[5] Many colonists remained neutral (no anti-war demonstrations in those days), and most probably valued stability over tumult, whether it was caused by the British or the rebels. Merchants rarely favor war. Many farmers, who would suffer economically from the war, did not support it. Certain religious denominations, such as the Quakers, did not support violent means of independence. We do know that around twenty-five thousand loyalists fought with the British army—many in the navy as well. Around one hundred thousand loyalists left the new United States once hostilities ended—which, as a number of historians have pointed out, was more than fled the far more populated France after its revolution.[6]

Once independence was achieved, however, almost all of the architects of our system agreed on one point: The concentration of power, even with "the people," is bad news. As it turned out, they were right. "People's Republics" have compiled an unimpressive record as sanctuaries of freedom. "People's Democratic Republics" are even worse. Strong currents of populism, if they had existed, might well have diverted the Revolution before it could coalesce into a long-lasting republic. Everyone knows that freedom must be safeguarded against the tyranny of ruling elites, but it takes more wisdom to realize that it must also be protected from abuse by our fellow citizens—

people who might be tempted to use democracy as a weapon for securing the submission of those who lack the electoral muscle to defend themselves.

The Constitution prohibits the United States government from granting titles of nobility, a provision that may reflect republican distaste for a traditional appurtenance of monarchy or a concern that future generations rely on meritocratic achievement rather than hereditary titles. Yet the Founders felt the need for some sort of counterbalance to the popular will. At the Virginia Ratifying Convention, Patrick Henry lamented the absence of a *class of nobility* in the new country because the nobility, historically, were a check upon the monarchy and the mob. Think of Magna Carta. It wasn't developed by Harvard-trained adjunct professors of constitutional law, and it certainly wasn't the product of peasants. It came from barons who were fed up with a tyrannical king and who had the power to stand up to him. In the same way, the medieval Church had served as a balance against royal prerogatives. For all its imperfections, it was the Church that imposed limits on the forms of warfare and the seasons for waging it, that ensured that peasants were relieved of work on feast days, that stood for the principle that men's spiritual affairs were beyond the competence of temporal powers. And Patrick Henry—for good reasons, it turns out—feared that presidents might sometimes act like kings.

So the Founders, mindful that revolutionaries can become a mob, built a government that was far more complex than the "executive-legislative-judicial" simplification taught in badly written textbooks. They assembled a purposefully byzantine system that constantly checks itself, a government that moves judiciously. The Senate rules that require, in effect, a supermajority for action are part of that tradition. The same goes for the process of amending the Constitution.

Two-thirds of each house of Congress must approve an amendment, and then three-quarters of the states. One layer of protection slathered atop another. Nothing is easy, and nothing should be crammed down our throats through fleeting populist support.

The Founders also carefully divided power between the federal government and the states, and they were not shy about saying that they meant the federal government to keep its hands off state prerogatives. "The powers not delegated to the United States by the Constitution," reads the Tenth Amendment, "nor prohibited by it to the States, are reserved to the States respectively, or to the people." The people—as individuals, not as some great god invested with the power to run roughshod over the rights of property and conscience. There is one other division of power in the Bill of Rights, though it's not usually thought of as a "check" or a "balance." It's the Second Amendment, the right to keep and bear arms. If all else fails, thought the Founders, it's back to square one, back to Lexington and Concord.

So the Founders finally established a republic. Its components were democratically elected, but it was a republic nevertheless. As John Marshall quickly conceded after admitting he "idolize[d]" democracy, "We contend for a well-regulated democracy."

The Founders understood better than most the difference between freedom and license, but almost everyone can intuit the distinction. Freedom is not merely doing what you please but taking responsibility for what you do. A man who does whatever his passions move him to do is not free, he is a slave. The exercise of true freedom, therefore, requires powers of self-control—*virtue*, as Aristotle would say. True freedom is compatible with the common good and does not impinge on the rights of others. License, on the other hand, is the corruption of freedom. It is freedom without responsibility. It is free rein to do as we feel whenever we feel like it regardless of the consequences.

License is incompatible with a healthy community and leads to moral chaos. Freedom thrives in a constitutionally sound republican government, while democracy is fertile ground for license.

The Federalist Papers reflect the Founding generation's awareness of the distinction, ignored today, between a republic and democracy. James Madison's *Federalist* No. 10—a rejection of government as the pure manifestation of the popular will—is the most skeptical statement about democracy by a Founding Father. Democracy, he says, is inadequate for the governance of anything but the smallest political entity. His great concern was the menace of "factions," by which he meant something close to what we would call "special interests"—not only the Koch Brothers and the National Rifle Association but environmentalist groups and other progressive lobbyists of all stripes. Madison did not condemn organized factions' seeking to advance particular interests; that was an inevitable consequence of liberty. Only a tyrannical government would prevent people with a common goal from joining forces to affect public policy.

A stable and just system of government, however, will minimize the ability of factions to appropriate the coercive government power at the expense of everyone else. Pure democracy, Madison warned, has no defense against such abuses. "A common passion or interest will, in almost every case, be felt by a majority of the whole; a communication and concert, results from the form of government itself; and there is nothing to check the inducements to sacrifice the weaker party, or an obnoxious individual. Hence it is that such democracies have ever been spectacles of turbulence and contention; have ever been found incompatible with personal security, or the rights of property; and have, in general, been as short in their lives as they have been violent in their deaths."

Madison, who once quipped that had "every Athenian citizen been a Socrates, every Athenian assembly would still have been the mob," believed that the sheer size of the United States, by diffusing democratic institutions, would protect it from the malign influence of factions. The variety of interests in such a diverse country would encourage moderation. "[I]f the proportion of fit characters be not less in the large than in the small republic," he wrote, "the former will present a greater option, and consequently a greater probability of a fit choice." As a result, representative democracy enjoys the benefit of "representatives whose enlightened views and virtuous sentiments render them superior to local prejudices and schemes of injustice."

However the advantages and disadvantages of democracy might have balanced out, the state of long-distance communication in the early days of the United States made direct democracy on a national scale impracticable. The entire population could not have cast votes on every single issue. In fact, one of the arguments in favor of the republican system was that it was suited to a large country. A functional democracy could, as a practical matter, extend no further than a city or county. Obviously, that wasn't good enough for a national government.

The logistical limitations on democracy have almost vanished in the information age, although the fiasco of the Obamacare website suggests that a national online system for voting on every issue would face considerable challenges. If you've ever watched C-SPAN, you can appreciate that most citizens wouldn't have the patience for the mundane business of debating and passing legislation, and it would hardly be an efficient use of their time. A prosperous society needs people working at productive jobs, not mulling over the fine points of interstate highway funding bills.

The deeper problem with democracy—in Madison's day as well as now—is that it doesn't offer sufficient protections for the rights of the minority. The Founders were concerned about mob rule, in which a majority—or even a highly organized and motivated minority—could use its voting muscle to enact laws that would be unfair to minorities. That's a danger under representative government as well, of course. The authors of our Constitution would be dismayed by how often it happens these days. But the representative republic offers far more protection against the abuse of state power to loot and pillage outnumbered voters.

New York governor Al Smith used to growl that the best cure for what ailed democracy was simply more democracy (which, as it has often been pointed out, is as ridiculous as saying the best cure for whatever ails communism is more communism). But let's examine democracy's record. In the 1830s, Tocqueville asserted that democracy and socialism were at odds. But it wasn't long before the twain began to meet. The rich got richer (sometimes honestly, sometimes not), and the not-so-rich got envious. Whether the latter called themselves populists or progressives or liberals or socialists or communists, they all professed an abiding faith in democracy, and the redistribution of wealth and the erosion of liberty were underway. "The ship of democracy, which has weathered all storms," said Grover Cleveland, "may sink through the mutiny of those on board."

The last conservative standard bearer of the Democratic Party before the populists took over at the end of the nineteenth century, Cleveland also declared, "True democracy ... seeks to lighten the burdens of life in every home and to take from the citizen for the cost of government the lowest possible tribute." But as democracy advanced in the Progressive Era, through direct primaries and the direct election of United States senators, a funny thing happened: the rich did not get poorer, but the government grew as rich as Croesus. The income tax started at 2 percent, and eventually its top marginal rate topped 90 percent. Sales taxes spread from state to state. Property taxes skyrocketed and forced people from their homes. Fees and business taxes proliferated.

Obliterating the last traces of states' rights hasn't improved democracy. True, the appeal to "states' rights" was often a means of depriving blacks of their civil rights (though one might ask if anything is more purely "democratic" than a lynch mob?), but they were also a haven for liberty when it was compromised in other states. Even Franklin Roosevelt recognized that. "The whole success of our democracy has not been that it is a democracy wherein the will of a bare majority of the total inhabitants is imposed upon the minority," he said in 1932, "but that it has been a democracy where through a division of government into units called States the rights and interests of the minority have been respected and have always been given a voice in the control of our affairs." But FDR's political heirs have dismantled this bulwark against democratic assaults on individual liberties.

———

The history of revolutions is not pretty. The French Revolution became the Reign of Terror, and soon enough there was a self-proclaimed emperor crowning himself. There was Spain in 1820, Russia in 1825, France again in 1830. In 1848 there were revolutions across the continent of Europe. And early in the twentieth century the most disastrous revolution of all befell Russia. Death and tyranny are the usual outcomes. Why was America's revolution uniquely successful? It helped immeasurably that the citizens of the new North American republic were the heirs of the freest and most stable political and legal tradition on earth. The conservative American revolutionaries adapted and reformed it, but they did not uproot it.

Sturdy institutions were not enough, however. America's experiment in self-government required self-governing people. They had to be adults. They had to be willing to govern themselves and to allow their fellow citizens the same freedoms they desired for themselves. They had to believe themselves accountable to a shared moral code, including the commandment "Thou shalt not covet thy neighbor's goods." And when they prayed "Lead us not into temptation," they had to include the temptation to use the power of the state to seize their neighbor's goods.

If Madison was the most articulate and influential voice against democracy at the Founding, the greatest student and theorizer of American democracy as it actually developed in the next generation was the French politician and philosopher Alexis de Tocqueville. Reading *Democracy in America* (published in two volumes in 1835 and 1840) doesn't make me think better of American democracy, but it does make me admire the people who lived under it. History has vindicated Tocqueville's admonitions about the political system he encountered in this country. He walked a razor's edge, praising the theory of democracy, which he admired, while identifying important problems in its practice.

In his letters, Tocqueville depicts a society with a multitude of races and religions but only one political ideology. Americans were united in their devotion to the country's democratic principles. In a society "lacking roots, memories, prejudices, habits, common ideas, a national character," there is a "faith" in the government and no "misgivings about the republic being the best of all possible governments." This uniformity of opinion seems on the surface to be a good thing, but it stifles those who question it.

Unlike the political philosophers of the ancient and medieval tradition, Tocqueville is not primarily concerned with the virtue of citizens and the pursuit of the common good. His concern is more immediate and more modest:

> Democratic governments will be able to become violent and even cruel in certain moments of great agitation and great dangers; but these crises will be rare and passing. ... After having thus taken each individual one by one into its powerful hands, and having molded him as it pleases, the sovereign power extends its arms over the entire society; it covers the surface of society with a network of small, complicated, minute, and uniform rules, which the most original minds and the most vigorous souls cannot break through to go beyond the crowd; it does not break wills, but it softens them, bends them and directs them; it rarely forces action, but it constantly opposes your acting; it does not destroy, it prevents birth; it does not tyrannize, it hinders, it represses, it enervates, it extinguishes, it stupifies, and finally it reduces each nation to being nothing more than a flock of timid and industrious animals, of which the government is the shepherd. I have always believed that this sort of servitude, regulated, mild and peaceful, of which I have just done the portrait, could be combined better than we imagine with some of the external forms of

liberty, and that it would not be impossible for it to be established in the very shadow of the sovereignty of the people.

It may not be a horrifying vision, but it is a vision of a state and a people gone vapid—uninspired and intellectually dead. Tocqueville describes a herd-like mentality that breeds a pervasive mediocrity in democracies—especially modern ones, in which those whose opinions go against the general consensus are cut off from many of society's benefits. In this sense, democracy becomes more than merely a political process; it becomes creed, faith, and religion. Its tenets are deemed nearly infallible, and its "justice" indubitable.

In his letters, Tocqueville observes Americans' preoccupation with their material self-interest, a trait that has by no means faded in the twenty-first century. "[T]he more one delves into the national character of Americans, the clearer it seems that they speak the value of all things of this world in the answer to only one question: 'How much money will it fetch?'" Although endeavoring to provide economically for oneself and one's family is no fault—and indeed for most people at most times it has been a consuming preoccupation—in a democracy like America's, where men share no "ancient mores, venerable traditions, deep rooted memories," they are forced to find meaning elsewhere. In this case, the "mercantile spirit" is the standard by which a man is judged, and not the nobler standard of classical virtue.

The defining feature of a society dedicated to the amassing of wealth is change—change for its own sake:

> As for instability of character, it shows through in a thousand places: an American takes something up, lets it drop, takes it up again ten times over during his lifetime; he is

constantly changing houses and embarking on new enterprises.... Moreover, change seems to him man's natural
state. And how could it be otherwise? Everything around
him is moving: laws, opinions, public functionaries, for-
tunes. Here the earth wears a new face every day.

This state of flux and impermanence gives the American democracy
a spirit that is "a far cry from the ancient republics." Those classical
states were bound to the past, to their shared history as a people, to
a common set of morals, virtues, and traditions that united them as
an abstract democratic constitution cannot do.

Tocqueville notes that the atomizing proclivity of democracy is
expressed in the American laws of inheritance. Before independence,
those laws followed the English principle of primogeniture, according
to which the bulk of a family's estate passes to the eldest male child.
Primogeniture, says Tocqueville, kept families unified, preserved
ownership, and fostered political stability since it furthered a sort of
aristocratic principle. In the wake of the Revolution, inheritance laws
were revised to provide equal division of estates. American democracy began with political equality and added equality of property at
the cost of a certain familial stability. Tocqueville warns that "our
families will disappear, possessions will pass into other hands, wealth
will be increasingly equalized." Continuity is not a priority in this
system, being replaced by the supreme good of "equality pushed to
the limit."

Tocqueville offers some cautious praise of democracy in addition
to his criticisms. But for all his admiration of what he found in America, he remains skeptical about its political future:

What I see in America leaves me doubting that government by the multitude, even under the most favorable

circumstances—and they exist here—is a good thing. There is general agreement that in the early days of the republic, statesmen and members of the two legislative houses were much more distinguished than they are today. The populace no longer chooses with such a *sure hand*. It generally favors those who flatter its passions and descend to its level. This effect of democracy, combined with what else I note about it—the extreme instability of all its elements, its absolute lack of perseverance in treating matters of state—reinforces my conviction that the most rational government is not the one in which *all concerned participate*, but the one directed by the most enlightened and moral classes of society.

It is hardly necessary to point out the striking timeliness of this nineteenth-century diagnosis of democracy's flaws. From Tocqueville's measured assessment of government by the multitude, let's turn now to a more recent critic.

The Founders assumed, wrongly it seems, that most of the electorate would take voting seriously. A people not seriously informed about the issues of the day or ignorant of basic economics will hand over its freedom and (usually somebody else's) money to the first smiling, silver-tongued demagogue. Modernity has made democracy less viable, not more. Over a century ago, the journalist Lincoln Steffens (no conservative or libertarian) wrote a groundbreaking book called *The Shame of the Cities*. He detailed the graft and corruption that infested big-city politics from New York to Philadelphia to Chicago to Pittsburgh to St. Louis. He told of union bosses who didn't mind the corruption as long as they got what they wanted and of businessmen who felt the same way. People blamed the politicians, the immigrants, the "system." Steffens dared to blame the real system.

He wrote, "'Blame us, blame anybody, but praise the people,' the politician's advice, is not the counsel of respect for the people, but of contempt. By just such palavering as courtiers play upon the degenerate intellects of weak kings, the bosses, political, financial, and industrial, are befuddling and befooling our sovereign American citizenship; and likewise they are corrupting it." The corruption of the government was the corruption of the people themselves, said Steffens.

"It has been observed that a pure democracy if it were practicable would be the most perfect government," wrote Alexander Hamilton before skewering the idea of purely democratic government: "Experience has proved that no position is more false than this. The ancient democracies in which the people themselves deliberated never possessed one good feature of government. Their very character was tyranny; their figure deformity." Hamilton, a true conservative, understood human nature. And human nature is why democracy can never work. Democracy makes demands of the mob. And coercion typically follows. "Democracy and socialism have nothing in common but one word, equality," said Tocqueville. "But notice the difference: while democracy seeks equality in liberty, socialism seeks equality in restraint and servitude."

CHAPTER 7

NO REVOLUTIONS

Certainly, gentlemen, it ought to be the happiness and glory of a representative to live in the strictest union, the closest correspondence, and the most unreserved communication with his constituents. Their wishes ought to have great weight with him; their opinion, high respect; their business, unremitted attention. It is his duty to sacrifice his repose, his pleasure, his satisfactions, to theirs; and above all, ever, and in all cases, to prefer their interest to his own. But his unbiased opinion, his mature judgment, his enlightened conscience, he ought not to sacrifice to you, to any man, or to any set of men living. These he does not derive from your pleasure; no, nor from the law and the constitution. They are a trust from Providence, for the abuse of which he is deeply answerable. Your representative owes you, not his industry only, but his judgment; and he betrays, instead of serving you, if he sacrifices it to your opinion.
—Edmund Burke, denouncing the "coercive authority" of instructions during his campaign for Parliament in 1774[1]

Can any of you seriously say the Bill of Rights could get through Congress today? It wouldn't even get out of committee.
—F. Lee Bailey, Newsweek, April 17, 1967

The great Anglo-Irish statesman and political philosopher Edmund Burke (1729–1797) spoke and wrote about direct majoritarian rule at a time when the world was first toying with the idea. A friend of the American colonies' cause in the British Parliament but an implacable opponent of the French Revolution and all it represented, Burke articulated the most important early critique of radical democracy, and his warnings, which were thoroughly vindicated, are worthy of renewed consideration.

Burke was a political conservative in the purest sense. He gave voice in Parliament to the colonists' demand for recognition of their rights as Englishmen, but he refused to embrace democracy as a universally valid system of governance. Burke gave an Aristotelian account of governments and traditions that were binding on individuals in their specific stations and societies. Like Aristotle he accepted the reality of human nature, and he warned that it is folly to transgress human nature in pursuit of utopia or to pander to the whims of the masses.

Almost all of Burke's writing focused on the events of his own time, the late eighteenth century—especially the revolutions in America and France. His most important work was *Reflections on the Revolution in France*, which began as private correspondence with a French friend and was published in 1790.

The key to Burke's thought about government, and democracy in particular, is the idea that respect for history, tradition, and human nature is the best guarantor of peace, stability, and freedom. In considering the French Revolution, the greatest political and cultural convulsion of his time, Burke addresses not the theory of democracy but the problems attending its implementation in France, though certain universal principles emerge from his analysis that the modern reader cannot help but notice.

The American Founding Fathers, especially James Madison, believed that the chief problem of democracy is faction, or a lack of unity, and many hand-wringing commentators of our own day share that view. Burke, however, believes that faction is conducive to general prosperity, that putting various interests at odds with one another benefits the whole. And indeed, this principle has become a fundamental feature of American politics.

The real problem with democracy, Burke saw, was the drift away from history, a drift that leads the people to imagine and then claim new "rights" rather than remain an innovative nation that relies on the inherited rules and institutions its ancestors developed to secure the morals and behavior requisite for ordered liberty.

The rallying cry of the French Revolution was "Liberté, égalité, fraternité!" It was the middle term, equality, that Burke was very careful with. Practical equality, he understood, is not reasonably possible:

> Believe me, Sir, those who attempt to level never equalize.
> In all societies consisting of various descriptions of citizens, some description must be uppermost. The levellers, therefore, only change and pervert the natural order of things: they load the edifice of society by setting up in the air what the solidity of the structure requires to be on the ground....

Burke would probably be critical of today's politicians who endlessly talk about "fairness" rather than opportunity. The pursuit of fairness has been the rationalization for many technocratic adventures in coercion that undermine freedom and try to override human nature. He argued that opposition to "equality" does not imply the denial of human rights. On the contrary, he favors "the real rights of men," the genuine benefits that traditional institutions and ways of life secure.

Burke emphasized genuine political communities with their particular histories, rights, and laws, passed down as an inheritance from generation to generation. There is no set of universal, abstract human rights existing in a vacuum, a perfect form or the ideal in which all earthly rights participate. Abstractions are treacherous. Against the "mazes of metaphysic sophistry" that weaken freedom's intrinsic relation to law and reduce power to "the will of a prevailing force," Burke argues that liberties cannot be divorced from their natural setting and the history of the people heir to them.

For Burke, the "fallible and feeble contrivances of our reason," an individual's reason merely, are to be complemented by the accumulated wisdom and experience of the ages, which has come down to us from our forebears. In the case of England, "[n]o experience has taught us that in any other course or method than that of a *hereditary crown* our liberties can be regularly perpetuated and preserved as our *hereditary right*." That is not to say that *all* nations require a hereditary monarchy, but that the practice of monarchy has thus far been the best safeguard for the peace and liberties of the English people.

This act of passing down has given Britain, says Burke, a constitution that "preserves an unity in so great a diversity of its parts. We have an inheritable crown, an inheritable peerage, and a House of Commons and a people inheriting privileges, franchises, and liberties from a long line of ancestors." Such a constitution is not the product of innovation, but of "the happy effect of following Nature, which is wisdom without reflection, and above it."

The revolutionaries in France, who demanded a radical equality among citizens, appealed to democracy as a form of government logically entailed by such equality. Burke has no more sympathy for the democratic ideologue than he has for the dogmatic egalitarian. In a nation "where popular authority is absolute and unrestrained, the people have an infinitely greater ... confidence in their own power.... [and] they are less under responsibility to the greatest controlling powers on earth, the sense of fame and estimation." Since the people as a whole rule, they lack a proper estimation of reputation and shame. They become indignant and proud because they are ultimately judges in their own case. Their shamelessness, "under a false show of liberty," seeks an " inverted domination, tyrannically to exact ... abject submission to their occasional will: extinguishing thereby, in all those who serve them, all moral principle, all sense of dignity, all use of judgment, and all consistency of character...."

Democracy, then, is the subjection of the state—and posterity— to "all the lust of selfish will." It is not grounded in tradition, in the handed down customs that buttress morality, but in momentary "floating fancies and fashions." Power resides not in time-tested institutions but in the will of the majority—it is found and lost in something fickle. Burke concludes: "A perfect democracy is therefore the most shameless thing in the world." When he encountered such a government in revolutionary France, he prudently used the occasion to warn the world against the dangers of radical abstraction and ignorance of human nature's weakness.

CHAPTER 8

"DEMOCRACY OF THE DEAD"

*Tradition means giving votes to the most obscure of all classes,
our ancestors. It is the democracy of the dead. Tradition refuses
to submit to the small and arrogant oligarchy of those who merely
happen to be walking about. All democrats object to men being
disqualified by the accident of birth; tradition objects to their
being disqualified by the accident of death.... I, at any rate, cannot
separate the two ideas of democracy and tradition; it seems
evident to me that they are the same idea.*
—G. K. CHESTERTON, ORTHODOXY

*Every generation laughs at the old fashions,
but religiously follows the new.*
—HENRY DAVID THOREAU, WALDEN

Like Burke, G. K. Chesterton's insight about tradition exposes one of the most serious problems with majoritarian democracy: its shortsightedness. If we fully give in to the will of the people today, it means we are giving in to the will of the people always. In modern America, we are all worshippers at Flip Wilson's "Church of What's Happening Now." Democracy, we believe, is about voting, majority rule, and responding to the electorate's immediate desires. In our confusion about the meaning of progress, we have no respect for the precedential authority of decisions made in the past. Even in the most fundamental questions of human life and society, the old and the established enjoy no presumption of truth but are the target of our scorn.

Gilbert Keith Chesterton (1874–1936), a debunker of false notions of progress, recognized the need to temper the ambitions of the affluent and influential do-gooders whose spirit of progress interferes and hinders more than it aids. But his critique of progress was not negative. Democracy, he argued, like any other human activity, will be fruitful only if it observes certain limits. Chesterton identified three principles that a self-governing people should observe.

The first principle is the primacy of tradition, which he famously called "the democracy of the dead." Tradition—the wisdom that our ancestors have "handed down," as the word literally means—grounds a society in age-old truths that are not the result of innovation for its own sake. "Change" is a popular political slogan, but it's an empty platitude. True progress is not always a rebellion against the past: "We have not any need to rebel against antiquity; we have to rebel against novelty," writes Chesterton.

The moral boundaries that tradition provides guide a society toward a genuine and deep freedom. Chesterton was suspicious of the merely popular, the fashionable, the evanescent. The "prince of paradox," Chesterton explained that true progress—change we can believe in, you might say—depends on permanent ideals, a "fixed vision" of good and evil, right and wrong. Real democracy is a faculty of a people that adheres to morality. Church and state, morality and politics are not antagonists in a real democracy. On the contrary, religion is the source of political principles.

Since democracy must be grounded in tradition, it functions better on a smaller scale, in which its citizens share the same traditions. It cannot be expected to work effectively if the number of participants is endlessly widening. The most successful and humane democracies will be found in fully functional local communities where the people share common bonds and borders.

Chesterton's second principle of democracy is that open and vibrant debate is a sign of a healthy society. The leaders of a sound democracy don't simply get together and get things done. They are inquisitive, boisterously intelligent, and questioning, and they don't submit to fads. Chesterton believed that successful democracy was an outgrowth of a society's taverns, where men frequently meet to discuss topics of importance. These discussions, these debates form citizens who participate with charitable and voracious minds in the government of the community, whatever their level.

Chesterton's third principle of democracy is responsibility. The individual is responsible for his actions, though the community should foster a climate of responsibility. Without personal responsibility, democracy collapses. Government, for Chesterton, is like writing a love letter or blowing your own nose: "these things we want a man to do for himself, even if he does them badly," and self-government must begin with governing oneself. A sense of individual responsibility allows the government to keep to its proper limits. "The most terribly important things," Chesterton says, "must be left to ordinary men themselves." American democracy in the early twenty-first century promotes the opposite. Each election provokes a new promise of giveaways and reliance on the state—and the occasion for more people to grab onto those promises.

The heart of Chesterton's political thought is the conviction that individual human beings matter. He recoiled from the worship of abstract "humanity." The next-door neighbor who is suffering should be the focus of our concern. "Man is something more awful than men."

Seven years before Chesterton's death at Beaconsfield, outside London, Alasdair MacIntyre was born in Glasgow. A Marxist in his youth, MacIntyre moved to the United States in 1969 and, over the course of a peripatetic academic career, became one of the leading philosophers in the world. Over many decades, he has constructed a powerful critique of the common notion that democracy is about self-determination, the right to choose and act according to one's desires, and that government exists merely to provide the skeletal framework within which individuals strive, unimpeded and unguided, toward their own independently chosen goals.

"'Politics' is the Aristotelian name for the set of activities through which goods are ordered in the life of the community," writes MacIntyre.[1] It is essentially a moral undertaking, it rises and falls based on the predominant moral convictions of the people. The origins of politics are in the moral and ethical life that is brought to fulfillment in and through the totality of human virtues. They are the foundation of politics.

The liberal individualism at the heart of American democracy is at odds with the classical conception of politics as a moral endeavor:

> For liberal individualism a community is simply an arena in which individuals each pursue their own self-chosen conception of the good life, and political institutions exist to provide that degree of order which makes such self-determined activity possible. Government and law are, or ought to be, neutral between rival conceptions of the good life for man, and hence, although it is the task of government to promote law-abidingness, it is on the liberal view no part of the legitimate function of government to inculcate any one moral outlook.

It's not that modern governments should propagate a particular moral system. MacIntyre makes a deeper point: the whole system of government, political life, and human society that is based on liberal individualism is irredeemably flawed; it is unsuited for the pursuit of genuine virtue and the good life, classically conceived. Without virtue, men are not truly free, and they cannot experience genuine community.

Since modern democracy, prescinding from an evaluation of human goods, is content with providing a framework within which individuals may exercise their self-determination, democratic government is deprived of a purpose. It has no means to encourage human flourishing. Democratic government is on the one hand categorical (universally applicable), abstract, and ignorant of human nature; on the other, it is ambivalent, without purpose, and amoral at best. Devoid of a grounding tradition, it cannot adequately and prudently direct its citizens to the best life for a given community.

This isn't an idea confined to conservatives. At least, it wasn't. Recently, I ran across an essay written by Bertrand Russell, a published column in the *New York Times Magazine* in 1951, titled, "The Best Answer to Fanaticism—Liberalism,"[2] in which the famed philosopher, mathematician, and leftist laid rules for living in a healthy democratic society.[3] From a liberal perspective, Russell—who, granted, was somewhat mercurial in his beliefs—went on to criticize the idea that change for change's sake was a positive force.

> The teacher who urges doctrines subversive to existing authority does not, if he is a liberal, advocate the establishment of a new authority even more tyrannical than the old. He advocates certain limits to the exercise of authority, and he wishes these limits to be observed not only when the authority would support a creed with which he disagrees but also when it would support one with which he is in complete agreement. I am, for my part, a believer in democracy, but I do not like a regime which makes belief in democracy compulsory.

Both Chesterton and MacIntyre recognize the weakness of democracy extended over a large territory. The larger the state, the more difficult it is to involve citizens effectively and intelligently in its governance. Like the Founding Fathers, MacIntyre argues that justice is best served in the local community, with its shared history, traditions, customs, and values. Indeed, democracy on the scale that it has reached in the United States may be untenable.

Our democracy is rent by increasing conflicts over rights and duties, conflicts that appear irreconcilable. Government on such a grand scale, where the values of people in one part of the country override by sheer political power those of people in another, cannot be reasonably maintained without some degree of tyranny. What is the ultimate purpose of democracy? What sort of lives are we meant to live? Our politicians seem to have lost a sense for the virtues that would bind us together in the quest for the common good: one where people cooperate out of a sense of place, habit, and right pleasures, as opposed to abstracted senses of justice that have little bearing on actual human lives.

Even nonbelievers, like me, can see the tendency of democracy to replace traditional beliefs with any number of insufficient and more despotic gods. And no god offers us more and delivers less than democracy itself. It would be rash to call for the dissolution of the political system at which Western culture has arrived after many centuries. But we are destroying the very things that made Western political society so fruitful. The heritage of place, people, and culture desperately needs shoring up. That's the most difficult aspect of politics.

PART III

THE COST

Don't be so gloomy. After all it's not that awful.
Like the fella says, in Italy for 30 years under the Borgias
they had warfare, terror, murder, and bloodshed, but they
produced Michelangelo, Leonardo da Vinci, and the Renaissance.
In Switzerland they had brotherly love—they had 500 years of
democracy and peace, and what did that produce?
The cuckoo clock. So long Holly.
—The Third Man (1949)

.

CHAPTER 9

MENCKEN AND THE MODERN BUGABOOS

We must not make a scarecrow of the law,
Setting it up to fear the birds of prey,
And let it keep one shape, till custom make it
Their perch and not their terror.
—SHAKESPEARE, *MEASURE FOR MEASURE*

Gracchus: *Fear and wonder, a powerful combination.*
Falco: *You really think people are going to be seduced by that?*
Gracchus: *I think he knows what Rome is. Rome is the mob.*
Conjure magic for them and they'll be distracted. Take away their
freedom and still they'll roar. The beating heart of Rome is not
the marble of the senate, it's the sand of the coliseum.
He'll bring them death—and they will love him for it.
—GLADIATOR

A mong early twentieth-century thinkers and writers who contributed to the debate over politics, government, and democracy, few are as prescient, cynical, funny, and worthy of our attention as Henry Louis Mencken. A son of Baltimore, Maryland, and a widely read journalist, he left an indelible mark upon American writing and politics. For good reason, he is still widely read and quoted today.

Mencken's lifelong fascination with the philosophy of Friedrich Nietzsche shaped his distrust of democracy and government by popular will. The fervent adoration of democracy was nearly universal in Mencken's America, but the great contrarian never shrank from caustic criticism of his countrymen's favored political philosophy. He believed it was indefensible to place the power of the state in the hands of those without the practical wisdom necessary to exercise it prudently and securely.

American politics, Mencken believed, valued the appearance of riches and moral rectitude above intelligence. Then as now, this disorder reflects the people's desire for "safety and security," a desire that is deeper in the American heart than the desire for virtue or freedom. Mencken returned to the theme of "safety and security" again and again, insisting on the baseness of the majority, who were preoccupied with satisfying their basest physical desires and were devoid of nobler aspirations.

Mencken, who accused the Prohibitionists of foisting "their brummagem cure-all upon the country under cover of the war hysteria," would find that little has changed today. The rhetoric of fear is a staple of both political parties. After 9/11, President Bush's press secretary, Ari Fleischer, warned Americans after the 9/11 attacks that they "need to watch what they say, watch what they do." In a faceoff over the budget, President Obama warned that congressional Republicans were pointing a "gun at the head of the American people" and threatening to "wreck the entire economy." Whether it's the president's science czar claiming that global warming could kill a billion people by 2020 or conservatives telling seniors that liberals want them to beg for their lives in front of "death panels," scaring constituents is an accepted way to build support.

Psychologists tell us that voters are keener to avoid what they fear than to seek what they desire, so political campaigns are festivals of negative advertising. Something like 80 percent of the presidential campaign ads in 2012 were negative. The inclination to rush for safety is powerful. After 9/11, Americans supported almost any government activity, however intrusive, that would keep us "safe," no matter how ineffective it might actually have been. Even a decade later, when the initial horror had faded, citizens had little interest in altering those policies, evaluating their success, or weighing the importance of safety over freedom. Every year since the attacks, government officials have warned us that terrorists are more potent, more creative, more resolved, and more dangerous—intimating that if only we knew what they did, we'd be curled up in our cellars crying. Democracy gives politicians the incentive to make life as scary as possible.

And more often than not, fear works. In 2013, the press was infuriated by revelations of the National Security Agency's internet and telephone surveillance programs, which scrutinized virtually every American. But the majority never supported efforts to curb the practice. Why not? According to a Google Survey CrunchGov analysis of public opinion on security issues since January 2006, approximately twice as many Americans have consistently valued efforts to "investigate terrorist threats" over efforts "not to intrude on privacy." And though 58 percent of the respondents to a CBS poll disapproved of the government's collection of information about "ordinary Americans," a majority of voters in a Pew/*Washington Post* survey approved of surveillance when told that the programs were supervised by the courts and intended to "investigate terrorism." Fear for our safety will almost always trump concern for basic liberties.

Partisanship adds a further element of unreality to calculations of safety in a democracy. When Gallup asked Americans in 2013 about government efforts to "compile telephone call logs and Internet communications," Republicans disapproved by a two-to-one margin. Democrats were largely ambivalent about the spying. Yet when Gallup asked almost the same question in 2006, during the presidency of George W. Bush, the responses were reversed, with Democrats showing high levels of skepticism. The only thing we have to fear, it seems, is what our chosen party tells us we should fear.

The politician, in Mencken's opinion, is merely "the courtier of democracy," whose sole aim is to "get and hold his job at all costs." He may at one time have had dignity, innocence, or principle, but he has exchanged them all for "the taste of boot-polish." He is ignorant, corrupt, and avaricious. Mencken, however, thought the British had avoided the complete debasement of their politics. In Great Britain, he thought, "outlawry and corruption of the best is checked by an aristocratic tradition—an anachronism, true enough, but still extremely powerful, yielding to the times only under immense pressure." The nobility—great families whose experience with political leadership spans generations and whose family honor is at stake—can best administer the country's affairs in a spirit of solemn duty. Aristocratic governors, moreover, enjoy the education suited to their role:

> The scholarship of Oxford and Cambridge, for example, can still make itself felt at Westminster, despite the fact that the vast majority of the actual members of the Commons are ignoramuses. But in the United States there is no aristocracy, whether intellectual or otherwise, and so the scholarship of Harvard, such as it is, is felt no more on

Capitol Hill than it is at Westerville, Ohio.... There is none of that interpenetration on the higher levels which marks older and more secure societies.

Mencken's touching faith in the benefits of an elite education was contradicted some years later by William F. Buckley Jr., who, unlike Mencken, actually had such an education and famously quipped that he would rather be governed by the first four hundred names in the Boston telephone directory than by the faculty of Harvard University.

"We are dependent for whatever good flows out of democracy," Mencken insisted, "upon men who do not believe in democracy." He believed he had demonstrated that the rule of the best is to the advantage of every class in the state. In a democracy, the general populace must be courted by politicians, but in a monarchy, the king is flattered by the courtier, who, in Mencken's words, "at least performs his genuflections before one who is theoretically his superior." The democratic politician, by contrast, at least vaguely aware of the mob's "dishonesty and stupidity," must debase and delude himself to believe that the mass of people are in fact "full of rectitude and wisdom." This perilous position requires public servants to follow the public will in everything, since the will of the mob is the perfect expression of justice and practical wisdom.

Menken, a commoner with a soft spot in his heart for nobility, was naïve about the morality and wisdom of the upper class. The idea of a titled American aristocracy would be anathema to voters, and for good reason. There is no static aristocracy, at least not for long, in a truly capitalistic society. In any case, it could be argued that we already have a de facto aristocracy, for despite the unpopularity of Congress as a whole, the reelection rate of its members is so high as to make them a permanent governing class. Their performance would inspire no one to make their aristocratic standing official.

American laws, in Mencken's words, are "invented ... by frauds and fanatics, and put upon the statute books by poltroons and scoundrels." Politics is not the candid discussion about issues but the jockeying for power to secure "private advantage." Laws in democracy are not inspired by the principles of justice and common sense but by the fear, aroused by demagogues, of persons and things that Mencken calls "bugaboos."

These bugaboos shape, for Mencken, the pattern and character of democracy. Politicians are able to turn the democrat's deep-seated desire for safety and security into fear of the bugaboos that will supposedly deprive him of his safety and security. Mencken observed this dynamic during World War I when suspicions were aroused against persons of German extraction, and he declared that "the business of law-making becomes a series of panics—government by orgy and orgasm." Fear rules in democratic politics. The people's apparent love of liberty is illusory:

> The truth is that the common man's love of liberty, like his love of sense, justice and truth, is almost wholly imaginary. As I have argued, he is not actually happy when free, he is uncomfortable, a bit alarmed, and intolerably lonely. ... The average man doesn't want to be free. He simply wants to be safe.

So Mencken posits an antinomy between democracy and genuine liberty. In a democracy, the mob sooner or later settles for a faux peace that is eerily akin to "a well-managed penitentiary." The "have-not" or "homo vulgaris"—Mencken's unflattering terms for the common man are reminiscent of Plato—cares more for the "warm, reassuring smell of the herd," for the base pleasures that his demagogical overlords parse out to him in accordance with "the delusion that he is the equal of his betters," than anything that a noble man would recognize as liberty.

Democracy erodes liberty as the mob restricts and persecutes its bugaboos. Eventually the majority turns on itself, regulating actions and delimiting thoughts. The superior individual, the man of intelligence, is beset on all sides in a democracy, preferring as he does the air of freedom, apart from the herd. It's no leap, then, for Mencken to claim, "The aim of democracy is to break all … free spirits to the common harness. It tries to iron them out, to pump them dry of self-respect, to make docile John Does of them." On the one hand, then, democracy is the expression of the free will of the masses, but on the other hand it is a manufactured response in which the manipulation of fear places groupthink above the genuine treacherousness of liberty. In Mencken's view, democracy promotes a cohesiveness that is based not on principle but on an uncritical reception of propaganda aimed at control and power. The dignity of man has no real place in this system, in spite of the rhetoric in praise of the common man. Dignity has been replaced with fear and envy.

Mencken blames American democracy's shortcomings on its Puritan origins. The mob's "politics is based upon the same brutal envies and quaking fears that lie under the Puritan ethic," by which he means the selfish desire to punish those who are seemingly "having a better time" by reducing them to the same misery as one's own. This Puritan ethic, Mencken finds, is the "theory behind Prohibition," which was the project of a small and fear-inebriated elite who inflicted their own petty hatred upon an entire country through propaganda and "dubious legislative experiments." Prohibition figures prominently in Mencken's discussion of democracy because it perfectly demonstrates how a self-righteous "elect" can seize control of the government of a society—"they are popular with the mob because they have a virtuous smack." Mencken would know exactly what to make of today's nanny state, which shreds our liberty to protect us not only from the vagaries of an unsafe world but from our own weaknesses. Crisis is the best shortcut to power, as Mencken warned his contemporaries.

Mencken uncovered a nasty secret of Puritanism and, by extension, the democratic system—a creeping and insidious distrust of other persons. Democracy's laws are not merely the weapons of fear and envy, they are sowers of distrust, instilling in the citizen a wariness of his fellows. Mencken came to the startling conclusion that the American people "are probably the least happy in Christendom." Common decency, a trait that he prized, is rare in an environment of fear and distrust, and relations among men sour. American society has to go in search of a substitute for decency, and where does it find it? In the pursuit and accrual of money, not for magnanimous purposes but for that core democratic value: security and safety, out of fear and envy.

Now, almost every political newcomer derides the environment of fear that Mencken describes. Those out of power have nothing to lose. When running for president in 2008, Obama regularly condemned the Bush administration's "politics of fear." Though he probably overstated Bush's fearmongering, he nevertheless had a point. Yet, as Mencken understood, fear is too potent a political weapon in democracy to allow for unilateral disarmament. As soon as Obama took office, it was nearly impossible to watch a political television show or read a newspaper without tripping over some Democrat comparing the 2007 recession to the Great Depression and warning of the calamitous consequences should citizens fail to support the president's economic program. Obama himself led the charge. "By now, it's clear to everyone that we have inherited an economic crisis as deep and dire as any since the days of the Great Depression.... And if nothing is done," he said while fighting for his stimulus plan, "this recession might linger for years.... Our nation will sink deeper into a crisis that, at some point, we may not be able to reverse." While the Republicans under Bush broadcast plenty of terrorist doomsday scenarios, liberals were no better, arguing that we'd all be hawking apples on a corner in our local shantytown if we didn't make their wildest Keynesian fantasies a reality. As Congress enacted a gargantuan pork-laden "stimulus," union bailouts, various other rescues, and a complete overhaul of the finance system, we debated who was at fault for the economic problems, but we rarely debated the merits of these plans.

Why not? Whether or not Obama's economic policies were good ideas, they were based on hysterical historical equivalence. And when Obama ran for reelection, with an actual record to defend, he summoned the fear of what might have been (which has the advantage of not being disprovable). So just as Bush won a second term by describing the existential threats from which he had saved the country, Obama was returned to power by virtue of the economic collapse that had been averted. The 2012 Obama campaign produced the film *The Road We've Traveled*—a masterpiece of counterfactual scaremongering—with the help of Academy Award winners Davis Guggenheim (*An Inconvenient Truth*) and Tom Hanks. The film lionizes one brave soul who, thrust by fate into historic turmoil and with no thought for his own well-being, sent hundreds of billions of your dollars to politically favored institutions. Without this particular man, implementing these particular policies, the United States would have surely crumbled. Tom Hanks's grave tone assures us this is true.

All this alarming theater garnered impressive results for Obama. The problem is that drama pushes us to make bad decisions based on bad history. As the economist Bradley Schiller pointed out, President

Obama's analogies to the Great Depression were "not only historically inaccurate" but "dangerous." At worst, he argues, the U.S. economy had shed 3.4 million jobs soon after the recession began, representing 2.2 percent of the labor force. A more appropriate comparison would have been November 1981 to October 1982, when 2.4 million jobs were lost, or 2.2 percent of the labor force. In 1930, during the Great Depression, the economy shed 4.8 percent of the labor force. In 1931, 6.5 percent. In 1932, 7.1 percent. Jobs were being lost at double or triple the rate of 2008–2009 or 1981–1982.[1] Every initiative of the Obama administration—including healthcare legislation, environmental subsidies, and tax hikes—became a "jobs bill," sold to a nation fearing economic collapse. American voters, who acted as if they were in the middle of a great depression, found themselves stuck with populist policies that produced unprecedented economic stagnation. If Mencken believed in an afterlife (which he didn't), he'd be looking down with grim satisfaction as the "booboisie" got exactly what they bargained for.

As democracy marches on, it leaves no space for honesty and genuine virtue, and it degenerates into widespread corruption. Its officials are bribed and sold, bought and bartered. And where there is corruption, there is power, for a "democratic state, indeed, is so firmly grounded upon cheats and humbugs of all sorts that they inevitably color its dealings with other nations." The United States, Mencken says, "is regarded universally to-day as a pious fraud—which is to say, as a Puritan."

To maintain the facade of liberty while continuing to feed at the trough of the state, democratic man begins to silence democracy's critics. Democracy becomes the state religion, Puritanism its philosophy, and bureaucrats its priests. In fact, writes Mencken, "democracy becomes a substitute for the old religion, and the antithesis of it." The government is "fidei defensor, before it is anything else, and its whole power, legal and extra-legal, is thrown against the skeptic who challenges its infallibility."

And so democracy continues to inbreed, fostering what is lowest in man. Lamenting the new hierarchy of values, Mencken writes:

> As the old aristocracies decline, the plutocracy is bound to inherit their hegemony, and to have the support of the nether mob. An aristocratic society may hold that a soldier or a man of learning is superior to a rich manufacturer or banker, but in a democratic society the latter are inevitably put higher, if only because their achievement is more readily comprehended by the inferior man, and he can more easily imagine himself, by some favor of God, duplicating it.

Culture therefore suffers in a democratic society, for its leaders are after nothing more than money. The high accomplishments of the "statesman, musician, painter, author, labor leader, scholar, theologian or politician" matter little in the face of the invented nobilities of wealth. The decrepitude of culture is the result not of aristocratic virtues—"a clean tradition, culture, public spirit, honesty, honor, courage—above all, courage"—but of their absence. Mencken longed for an aristocratic class with real power to shape society, freed from the vexations and fearmongering of the demagogues and from the banal tastes of the plutocrat.

A noble class, moreover, is an antidote for democracy's foolish optimism about progress. Mencken finds the "sweet democratic axiom" that "progress is illimitable and ordained by God—that every human problem, in the very nature of things, may be solved" to be repugnant. He yearns for a disinterested aristocracy, which with courage and benevolence will reform democracy, separating "the good that is in it theoretically from the evils that beset it practically, and then try to erect that good into a workable system."

Mencken could be philosophical about the paradoxes of democracy: it aims to give men liberty but suspends it; it claims its mandate to rule from the people but violently polices them; it is based on the rule of law but judges decide which laws to obey and which to neglect. Despite his harsh tone, Mencken found some amusement in the democratic cavalcade: "Does [democracy] exalt dunderheads, cowards, trimmers, frauds, cads? Then the pain of seeing them go up is balanced and obliterated by the joy of seeing them come down.... Is rascality at the heart of it? Well, we have borne that rascality since 1776, and continue to survive."

CHAPTER 10

DEMOCRACY: AN ECONOMIC WRECKING BALL

Just tell 'em you're gonna soak the fat boys and forget the rest of the tax stuff ... Willie, make 'em cry, make 'em laugh, make 'em mad, even mad at you. Stir them up and they'll love it and come back for more, but, for heaven's sakes, don't try to improve their minds.
—ALL THE KING'S MEN

Anything popular is populist, and populist is rarely a good adjective.
—BRIAN ENO

The most consequential threat to economic prosperity isn't the big banks or China or the loss of manufacturing jobs. It's us. Populism—democracy's rapacious half-wit progeny— pits "the people" against a presumed privileged "elite," with economically crippling results.

In his book *The Myth of the Rational Voter: Why Democracies Choose Bad Policies*, the economist Bryan Caplan points to a number of irrational positions voters take in the realm of economics that propel destructive policies. One is anti-market bias, which refers to our "tendency to underestimate the economic benefits of the market mechanism." Here voters see themselves as victims of the marketplace, rather than participants. It is the irrational belief that most corporations and small businesses are selfish rent seekers out to cheat the consumer. Another bias is our "tendency to underestimate the economic benefits of interaction with foreigners." Here, foreigners are seen as antagonists rather than a source of healthy economic competition that is essential for economic growth. Another is the "make-work bias," which refers to our "tendency to underestimate the economic benefits from conserving labor." This is a fear of productivity.

What is populism? Well, the most basic definition is "a political doctrine that supports the rights and powers of the common people in their struggle with the privileged elite." Populism typically favors the truths and morality of the masses and offers to hand over power to the people in the struggle against what they see as the privileged upper class—no matter what those ideas entail, including coercion of minorities. "Democracy is the road to socialism," Marxists believe, and progressive populism is about as socialistic as a person can get in the United States. Throughout American history there has been a tension between the elites and upstarts, the old timers and the new comers, the progressive thinkers and the traditionalists. This battle of old and new is a healthy and necessary component to a healthy society. There seems to be a reticence these days to admit that new things can be harmful or imprudent. Today "populism" exists both on the left and right, it is aimed at plodding and corrupt institutions—big government and big business. For our purposes populism will indicate the traditional progressive populist movement.

Populism is when Senate Majority Leader Harry Reid says, "A party that stands with Wall Street is a party that stands against families and against fairness." Really? You know Wall Street; it *lives* to destabilize the family unit, right? That's why nearly 50 percent of households own some form of equities, and 21 million households own individual stocks outside any employer-sponsored plan. Are all companies whose stocks are traded on Wall Street—8,500 on the New York Stock Exchange and 3,200 on the NASDAQ—working together against kids and fairness? Probably not. Is a "party that stands with Wall Street" really "a party that stands against families and against fairness," or does it support American businesses that provide jobs and whose stocks provide a way for families to invest and maximize savings?

Have many Wall Street firms engaged in shady dealing and hurt American families? Of course they have. The problem with most populist ideas is that they are built on fear and envy, and democracy gives them power.

You can see the attraction of populist ideas for politicians. They can frighten voters by alleging a conspiracy between billionaires and foreigners to steal their jobs. They can identify with the struggles of the Average Joe by wagging their finger at some callous corporation that is shutting down a factory. They can bewail "outsourcing"—even if as a matter of economic fact outsourcing is merely another advance in the division of labor that improves economic efficiency and in the process creates more wealth and *better jobs*. It is certainly fair to debate the benefits of international labor and trade, but we don't. In democracy, it's far easier to demonize.

Yet, it is a political imperative to continue to push the narrative that America is on the precipice of disaster. That government, led by whichever politician is running at the time, will fulfill the promise of America. Here is how President Obama put it during his most recent campaign: "It is our unfinished task to restore the basic bargain that built this country—the idea that if you work hard and meet your responsibilities, you can get ahead, no matter where you come from, no matter what you look like, or who you love."

Actually, there is no such bargain, nor has there ever been, so there is nothing to restore. It seems that this is the sort of merit-based guarantee of success that politicians like to make. There is no assurance that if you work hard and meet your responsibilities—whatever Obama believes those duties may entail—that you're going to get ahead in life. In real life plenty of good people fail and plenty of terrible people succeed. The Fairness Bunny only exists in politics.

In the 2012 campaign, President Obama focused his attacks on Mitt Romney and the idea that free international trade was stealing Americans' jobs and undermining domestic economic development. When the *Washington Post* reported that Romney, while head of Bain Capital in the mid-1990s, had invested in companies that were not simply outsourcing but were "pioneers" in shipping jobs overseas, Obama's campaign tagged the Republican nominee as the "out-sourcer-in-chief." And after Romney aides made the foolish tactical error of trying to explain a factual distinction during a political campaign (the last thing we want), Obama, who understands the force of populism as well as anyone, joked that they "tried to clear this up by telling us that there was a difference between 'outsourcing' and 'offshoring.' Seriously. You can't make that up."

Actually, Mr. President, there *is* a difference, and it's rather important. Obama, and scores of other candidates, knew that to the average anxiety-ridden voter, "outsourcing" and "offshoring" *sounded* the same, and that's good enough in a democracy. ("Outsourcing" is when a company contracts with an outside party to do work on the company's behalf. "Offshoring" is when a company takes a function out of the country and moves it elsewhere.) By outsourcing, companies can remain competitive, more productive, and more profitable, and more profitable businesses often create higher-paying jobs in the United States. Consumers in turn benefit from the lower costs of products and services that outsourcing makes possible. They can spend that savings on products and services they value. That's a lot to explain, and voters will never like the sound of it. So rather than allow the marketplace shake-out, our instincts demand that government ameliorate the natural churn of economic growth.

And so politicians will rarely, if ever, talk about the benefits of these wholly practical ideas. Politics demands that we pretend that Adam Smith never lived. But for the sake of argument, let's concede that outsourcing is a quantifiable problem, that it's destroying the American worker whose job is "shipped" to some Asian nation. Knowing full well that protectionist ideas have often decimated economies, what do Democrats—and many Republicans, who have ridden this protectionist hobbyhorse—propose we do? They appease voters with half-measures that are enough to get them reelected but hurt the economy. There is enough pent up democratic demand to force companies to keep unsustainable jobs in the country. One of the components of Obama's proposed "jobs plan" was punitive tax increases on corporations that "ship jobs overseas." Most polls find big majorities in favor of hiking corporate taxes, even though the United States is already one of the most aggressive nations in taxing profit earned abroad, and such taxes will simply be passed along to consumers.

In economic policy, what *feels* right and what *is* right diverge more than people imagine. Nothing illustrates this truth better than the minimum wage. Though the consensus has contracted somewhat over the past few years, most economists agree that raising the minimum wage either destroys jobs or does little to create more of them. And very few economists argue that the minimum wage alleviates poverty.

Left to democracy, however, the minimum wage may one day be $20, $30—why not $40? Support for the minimum wage has hovered between 70 and 80 percent since Gallup began asking about it a few decades ago. The last time I checked, seven in ten Americans would raise the minimum wage to $9 per hour, and only 27 percent would try to stop such an increase. A $9 minimum wage, which Obama proposed in his 2013 State of the Union address, wins the support of 90 percent of Democrats and liberals and two-thirds of independent voters. Even conservatives "tilt slightly in favor," according to Gallup. And when Obama's approval ratings started to wane, he reportedly began to consider supporting a Democratic bill that would raise the federal minimum wage to $10.10 and link future increases to inflation.

The economist Thomas Sowell has spent thirty years explaining why minimum wage laws harm the young and unskilled:

> Advocates of minimum wage laws usually base their support of such laws on their estimate of how much a worker "needs" in order to have "a living wage"—or on some other

criterion that pays little or no attention to the worker's skill level, experience or general productivity. So it is hardly surprising that minimum wage laws set wages that price many a young worker out of a job.

The same impulse that makes people stand behind a feel-good measure like the minimum wage in spite of the overwhelming evidence of its harm also leads them to lament rising productivity, even though doing more with less is necessary for economic growth. Warning that "[t]here are some structural issues with our economy where a lot of businesses have learned to become much more efficient with a lot fewer workers," the president who calls himself "the change we have been waiting for" complains, "You see it when you go to a bank and you use an ATM, you don't go to a bank teller, or you go to the airport and you're using a kiosk instead of checking in at the gate."[1] Another visionary, sometime congressman Jesse Jackson Jr., offered the equally sophisticated argument that the iPad was "probably responsible for eliminating thousands of American jobs." If we read our books, newspapers, and magazines on tablets, Jackson wonders, what will happen to "all the jobs associated with paper"? (As I write, he is serving a thirty-month prison sentence—not, unfortunately, for crimes against reason.)

Increasing productivity, of course, is not a structural problem. Efficiency drives growth and improves the quality of goods and services—along with our lives. Technology is a job producer. Nevertheless, there is no denying that productivity exacts a real and personal toll on many Americans. In his classic book *Capitalism, Socialism and Democracy*, the economist Joseph Schumpeter popularized the term "creative destruction"—a "process of industrial mutation that incessantly revolutionizes the economic structure from within, incessantly destroying the old one, incessantly creating a new one." Simply put, creative destruction occurs when something new (iPad) kills something older (newspaper). Though populist rhetoric will never warm up to the idea of creative destruction, consumers in their everyday lives almost always do. It's why you now might buy a book—perhaps this one—on an electronic device rather than in a bookstore. It's why you get most of your news from the internet, and why many of you can purchase three-thousand-square-foot palaces in the suburbs that would have been unimaginable for most everyone a couple of generations ago.

The incompatibility of what we demand of politicians and what we demand of our economy results in a huge mess. We love technological advances, but democracy demands emotionally pleasing but unsustainable "job-saving" measures like bailouts, subsidies, and "stimulus." Today's Luddite wages war on an abstraction called "Wall Street," where some players act illegally and recklessly and some undermine healthy competition. But the vast majority of companies devise new technologies, services, and products that make modern life possible. If they don't, they fail. The modern-day Luddite can demonize "big oil," "big food," and "big pharma" all day long. He can decry profit as if Satan himself invented the notion. Yet when the multinational firm GlaxoSmithKline announces, as it did recently, that it has developed the first effective vaccine for malaria, you can bet that such a breakthrough never would have happened in a system where productivity diminishes. And if the vaccine is successful, the company will have done more good for the world than a million demonstrations against the evils of capitalism.

Donald Boudreaux, a professor of economics at George Mason University, has told me that there's "no reason to suppose that 3D printing poses a greater threat to overall jobs and economic opportunity than did power looms of centuries ago." We're richer and better educated, we have access to more information, and we travel more easily and cheaply than our early-industrial ancestors. "Also," he goes on, "capital markets are more advanced. So I can't think of a good reason why people today are less able than were people in the past to deal with creative destruction."

The responsibility for America's stagnating jobs market is more likely to rest with our populist economic policies than with the malign forces of "Wall Street." The systemic coddling of government-favored corporations has finally taken a toll on job growth. The government's habit of rescuing rotting corporations from their well-deserved fates—companies like AIG or General Motors—is obstructing creative new enterprises. An administration that fosters a "fairer" economy over an innovative one is hampering job creation.

Question: Which is more likely to undermine economic activity: Twitter or the Obama administration's twelve thousand new pages of regulations?

"The temptation is to blame markets if, for ordinarily workers, creative destruction is more destructive than creative," Boudreaux observes. "But perhaps the accumulation over the years of capital-market regulations, labor-market and occupational-licensing regulations, consumer products–market regulations, and the hidden taxes (e.g., Obamacare) that attend many of these regulations are, unlike in the past, finally indeed preventing markets from doing what markets would otherwise naturally do: create new opportunities for workers displaced by technology."

The truth is that innovation doesn't occur where and when pundits, computer scientists, technocratic presidents, or voters expect. We can lament that Kodak employed 140,000 people yesterday while Instagram employs only thirteen today. But the innovation of hydraulic fracturing—the process of injecting water, sand, and chemicals to free gas trapped in rock—will create many millions of new jobs.

Scientific consensus finds the process completely safe. Yet fracking is a politically disfavored industry, so we erect more and more roadblocks in its path. A 2013 Bloomberg poll found that 66 percent of Americans wanted to slow down production by piling more regulatory burdens onto perhaps the most regulated industry in the nation. Polls in California and New York reveal sky-high opposition to fracking. The administration shows no interest in fostering that innovation, but it will divert billions of dollars every year to prop up unproductive farms and "clean" energy start-ups.

Americans tend to romanticize bygone days when a lunch-pail-toting union laborer headed off each day to a high-paying factory job and made something tangible for consumers. Now that those jobs are gone, we need something to blame, and democracy obligingly supplies our target: foreign workers. Fear, churned in the never-ending political cycle, thus insures that bad ideas like protectionism will always have bipartisan support.

In 2010, when the Democratic-controlled House of Representatives passed the Currency Reform for Fair Trade Act—an expansion of the infamous Depression-instigating Smoot-Hawley Tariff Act—ninety-nine Republicans, self-proclaimed champions of the free market, voted for it. This kind of bill gets wide public support. A *Wall Street Journal* poll found that 50 percent of voters believe free-trade agreements have hurt the United States, up from 46 percent three years earlier and 32 percent in 1990. (This poll also found that 90 percent of Republicans agree that "outsourcing" is one reason for our economic problems.)

The Obama Commerce Department continued the protectionist follies in 2012 by slapping tariffs on Chinese solar panels. There was virtually no public backlash. The tariff kept the price of solar panels high, and many economists warned that it would provoke a trade war. Sure enough, the Chinese government began enforcing tariffs on American polysilicon, an essential ingredient in the production of solar panels. The sorry but utterly predictable results were apparent in a 2013 *Washington Post* report on Michigan-based Hemlock Semiconductor, one of the leaders in the field, which laid off hundreds of workers in anticipation of the trade restrictions. The United States then threatened retaliation.

No matter how many times history drives a stake through the heart of protectionism, it returns like the undead in a horror movie. Free trade is abstract and counterintuitive, so there are few policies more difficult to defend in the democratic forum. There are also few policies more demonstrably correct.

Voters will usually believe the worst without much prodding. Pew found in November 2013 that 48 percent of Americans believed that China was the world's top economic power. (Only 31 percent correctly identified the United States as the preeminent power, with an economy nearly *three times* the size of China's.) Another Pew survey from 2012 found that 47 percent of us consider China's growth a "bad thing" for the United States. A CNN poll found that 58 percent of us believe that China's "wealth and economic power" are a threat to the United States. I'm certain our relationship with China is layered with complexity and fraught with danger. But why would we fear the aspect of China's ascendancy—its "wealth and economic power"— that poses the least threat to the United States? Unlike ideological clashes, economic competition can be mutually beneficial. A country with a robust economy is typically free and doesn't look kindly on radical behavior. Suicide bombers rarely drive top-of-the-line BMWs. But democracy breeds fear. Which candidate will declare on the hustings, "Ladies and gentlemen, manufacturing jobs have declined in the past twenty years because there has been an incredible rise in the productivity of the American worker. Congratulations. The output at U.S. factories was 37 percent higher in 2009 than it was in 1993.

Yes, it has doubled since 1970! You're just going to have to find something else to do. Good luck!"

Just as we fear the unknown, we tend to protect what we know—even if it no longer works. The most notorious example of this tendency is the bailouts of the American automobile manufacturers, but populist economics has led the government to prop up countless other industries. Coddling the unproductive is a time-honored and bipartisan tradition in Washington. Sometimes it is driven by romanticism about certain aspects of American life, as in the case of agricultural policy, which has been a disaster since the 1930s.

You may recall a Super Bowl commercial for Dodge Ram pickups called "God Made a Farmer." It was a beautiful ad, featuring still shots of hardscrabble life in the American Midwest and a speech by Paul Harvey celebrating the noble farmer: "God said, 'I need somebody willing to get up before dawn, milk cows, work all day in the fields, milk cows again, eat supper, then go to town and stay past midnight at a meeting of the school board." Now, school board meetings may be as tedious as ever, but with the technological advances we've seen in agriculture and the remarkable boom in productivity, God probably doesn't need the same level of commitment from the farmer anymore. This romantic vision of agriculture—in movies, literature, ads, and politics—makes it nearly impossible to shoo the industry away from the government trough.

Farmers, believe it or not, are not Mother Teresa; they get paid for what they do. There are other jobs just as vital to the nation as farming, many of them in industries struggling to survive, many of them entailing far more risk, yet agriculture is the only vocation I can think of in the private sector that is treated as if it were a form of patriotism.

"If you want to become rich," Jim Rogers, the noted investor, once said, "become a farmer." Small farms are dying because they can't compete with the productivity of larger competitors, a reality that many other industries wrestle with—and from which consumers inevitably benefit. But even if farm subsidies were intended to alleviate rural poverty and disparity within the industry, why do most subsidies go to commercial farms with average incomes of $200,000 and $2 million? The economist Robert Samuelson recently pointed out:

> Symbolic of the debate we're not having about government's size and role—the essence of the deficit problem— is the future of farm subsidies. Running $10 billion to $15 billion annually, they don't do much good. For starters, they haven't saved small farms. Since the 1930s, when subsidies began, the number of farms is down 70 percent. Nor do farmers need subsidies to stay profitable. Farmers' income for 2011 and 2012 ($135 billion and $133 billion, respectively) were the highest and second-highest ever and would have been without subsidies.

Taxpayers spend about $7 billion a year on crop insurance alone, the largest farm subsidy, as if the industry had the God-given right to operate in certainty. The Department of Agriculture hands out between $10 and $30 billion in cash to farmers every year, depending on the vagaries of the world around them. Ten percent of the farmers collect 75 percent of the subsidies. More than 90 percent of agriculture subsidies go to the producers of just five crops—wheat, corn, soybeans, rice, and cotton. Government subsidizes almost none of the fruits and vegetables we eat (also grown under the threat of unpredictable weather) or the flat screen TVs we watch (also produced in a highly competitive marketplace), yet you can find any of them without worrying too much about serious fluctuations in price.

I've got nothing against farmers, but when we implement price controls and impel Americans to buy things like ethanol, even though the policy does nothing to satisfy our energy needs or to curb pollution, we only distort the price of crops and increase food costs for consumers. Perhaps I'm overstating the influence of popular sentiment, but I can't help believing that our distorted agricultural policy has something to do with public perception. Why haven't these policies been substantively altered in seventy years? Because in red states, populist notions about agriculture won't allow it.

Despite the economic stagnation of the Obama years, American workers and consumers are better off than they were in 1980 thanks to advances in technology and productivity. But there is one characteristic of capitalism that will never change, even after we have shaken off the Great Recession: some of us will always have more than others.

Economic inequality is a valid concern (even if pundits and politicians overplay the gap between rich and poor). But you can't go anywhere on the internet these days without tripping over a fevered denunciation of the "explosion" of inequality, the dark smog of capitalistic excess that is choking the life out of this unjust nation. Populism distorts our understanding of the problem and how we try to deal with it.

Yet wealthy people—at least in a free-market society like ours—are not usually wealthy because they took something from the poor or from government. Their wealth doesn't keep anyone else from being wealthy. And the wealthy did not create our debt; government did. Government is immune from the consequences of its failed "investments." Not so you or I. Moreover, if the rich get richer, no one has to become one penny poorer. The childish idea that the economy is a zero-sum game might appeal to the populist sentiments of the so-called "99 percent," to the envy of some others, or to the emotions of many who are struggling through this terrible economy, but in the end, it doesn't stand up to the most rudimentary inspection.

The notion that runaway income disparity is destroying the American middle class has been repeatedly debunked. Yes, some are getting *super* rich, but many others are getting richer as well, just at a slower pace. James Pethokoukis of the American Enterprise Institute points out that even Congressional Budget Office "data show real median after-tax household income (half of all households have income below the median, and half have income above it) grew by 35 percent over the past three decades." Over the past half-century, in fact, the wages of the middle class have constituted a remarkably consistent share of gross domestic product. And the most important contradiction of the protesters and progressives is that the poorest 5 percent of Americans are still richer than nearly 70 percent of the rest of the world. And they enjoy far greater opportunity to improve their situation.

A 2007 Treasury Department study showed that 58 percent of households that were in the bottom quintile in 1996 had moved to a higher level by 2005, and of households in the top 1 percent during the same period, more than 57 percent dropped to a lower income group. As Reason Foundation's Shikha Dalmia explains, "New data from the University of Chicago's Steven Kaplan shows that, despite government bailouts, in 2008 and 2009 the adjusted gross income of the top 1 percent—a disproportionate number of whom work in the financial industry—fell to 1997 levels." These numbers show great mobility, upward and downward, and it's why "class" as a political wedge issue hasn't typically held as much traction in the United States as it has elsewhere.

But let's concede that, thank goodness, there will be some inequality as long as we are a largely meritocratic society. But even if disparity were corroding our society, as many would have you believe, what's the remedy? Are Americans prepared to take on a massive social engineering project in which politicians, commissars, and czars make biased and arbitrary decisions about who deserves what and who doesn't? Sometimes it seems that we are. This sort of democratically determined central economic administration has been attempted all over the world, resulting in varying degrees of economic tragedy. Populist economic rule, of course, is impossible. And it leads to real trouble.

CHAPTER 11

GRIDLOCK
SAVES
THE REPUBLIC

*A perfect democracy is, therefore,
the most shameless thing in the world.*
—EDMUND BURKE, *REFLECTIONS ON THE REVOLUTION IN
FRANCE*

*Though liberals do a great deal of talking about hearing
other points of view, it sometimes shocks them to learn that
there are other points of view.*
—WILLIAM F. BUCKLEY JR., *UP FROM LIBERALISM* (1959)

O
n December 14, 2012, twenty-year-old Adam Lanza mas-
sacred twenty children and six adults at Sandy Hook Elementary School in the village of Sandy Hook in Newtown,
Connecticut. As is always the case with these kinds of heartbreaking
tragedies, a national debate over guns broke out, pitting gun control
advocates against Second Amendment supporters. Through the
process, President Barack Obama struggled to wrap his head around
the "unimaginable" idea that Congress may "defy" the American
people and stop a vote on a gun control package compromise in the
Senate. The notion, he says, resists the "overwhelming instinct of the
American people" after the massacre in Newtown to pass gun control
legislation.

Well, the unthinkable happened. The Senate's sweeping gun legislation came up short on the votes required to move forward. And
despite all the idealistic calls for passage and despite the fact that many
pundits and advocates seem to believe that something should be law
simply because "the vast majority of Americans" support it, not every
issue deserves a majoritarian decision.

To begin with, whether Democrats like it or not, this issue concerns the Constitution—written to override the impulses of democracy. That's not to say that expanding background checks or banning
"assault rifles" would be unconstitutional (though you may believe
they both should be), it's to say that when you begin meddling with
protections explicitly laid out in the Founding document, a 60-vote
threshold that slows down stampeding legislators is the least we
deserve. And we probably deserve a higher threshold.

The Founding Fathers worried that "some common impulse of
passion" might lead many to subvert the rights of the few. It's a rational fear, one that is played out endlessly. Obama, who understands
how to utilize public passion better than most, flew some of the

Newtown families to Washington for a rally, imploring Americans to put "politics" aside and stop engaging in "political stunts." This is, by any measure, a preposterous assertion coming from a *politician* piggybacking on tragic events for political gain. It would have been one thing, I suppose, if the gun control legislation written in the aftershock of a gruesome massacre had anything to do with the topic at hand. But what senators came up with would have done nothing to stop the shooter in Newtown—or the similarly horrific one in Aurora, Colorado. Passions can be aggravated by events, but in this case, events have little to do with the policy at hand.

But generally speaking, it'd be nice if Congress occasionally challenged the vagaries of American majority "instinct." Though it might seem antithetical to their very existence, politicians should be less susceptible to the temporary whims, ideological currents, and fears of the majority. Theoretically, at least, elected officials' first concern is the Constitution. And if the need for gun control is predicated chiefly on the polls taken immediately after a traumatic national event, they have a perfectly reasonable justification to slow things down. In fact, if Washington internalizes the 60-vote threshold as a matter of routine, voters should be grateful. Considering Washington's propensity to politicize everything and its increasingly centralized power (what your healthcare looks like is now up for national referenda, for instance), this might be the only way left to diffuse democracy.

As we all know, in Washington, the greatest crisis is not getting everything you want. Elected officials whine about their inability to "get things done" because of unprecedented "gridlock." It's always the fault of obstructionists who put partisan politics before the people's business. The Founders might have erected an elaborate system of checks and balances to impede the gush of power, bad ideas, and passions, but the exigency of overcoming "gridlock"—the "fierce urgency of now," as Obama might say—trumps all other concerns. The most alarming thing about modern politics is not that elections don't have consequences but that they have too many.

Any residual federalist barrier that slows the pace of majoritarian legislation is intolerable, the politicians and pundits scream. Polarization in Washington is a natural safeguard against one party's fundamentally changing the institutions of the country, but we are schooled to lament it.

Like judicial barriers. Even the Supreme Court isn't immune to political forces that pressure us into adhering to hyper contemporary thinking. In 2010, for instance, the Supreme Court struck down part of a federal law regulating campaign spending by corporations and unions in *Citizens United v. Federal Election Commission*. For some, myself included, the decision was a clear victory for free speech (more on that later). President Obama didn't see it that way. We can disagree about the veracity and rightness of decisions. The Supreme Court, a collection of human beings, makes mistakes like everyone else. But Obama took it one step further in his State of the Union and personally attacked the Supreme Court—with a mass of senators and congressmen jumped up to express their approval at the spectacle. Obama began his attack with the words "with all due deference to separation of powers"—which was the very thing he sought to undermine.

Peter G. Verniero, a former justice on the New Jersey Supreme Court, told the *New York Times* that, the "court's legitimacy is derived from the persuasiveness of its opinions and the expectation that those opinions are rendered free of partisan, political influences. The more that individual justices are drawn into public debates, the more the court as an institution will be seen in political terms, which was not the intent of the founders."[1]

The public attack on the court was also a way to influence the referees in the future. President Obama would return to lecture the American people leading up to the Supreme Court decision regarding the "individual mandate," the mechanism that coerces all Americans to participate in Obamacare. Leading up to the decision, which had the potential to sink the entire healthcare reform bill, the president reminded everyone that democracy, rather than checks and balances, was destined to run Washington: "I'd just remind conservative commentators that, for years, what we have heard is, the biggest problem on the bench was judicial activism, or a lack of judicial restraint, that an unelected group of people would somehow overturn a duly constituted and passed law. Well, this is a good example, and I'm pretty confident that this court will recognize that and not take that step."[2]

In reality, it was a frontal attack on the core of the nation's most vital institution. Surely a former constitutional law professor understands the outrageousness of denying the top court the ultimate power to decide the meaning of the Constitution. The Supreme Court's job is not to make law but to gauge the constitutionality of it—even if, as the president said, it means overturning "a duly constituted and passed law." What other type of law should the court overturn? If the Supreme Court—or, as Obama likes to point out an "unelected group of people"—had knocked down Obamacare's individual mandate, it would not have been taking an "an unprecedented, extraordinary step of overturning a law that was passed by a strong majority of a democratically elected Congress."

Fact is, a "strong" majority did not support Obamacare. It was passed using parliamentary maneuvering, without the vaunted consensus of democracy, in a Democratic Congress. But even if 99 percent of Americans supported it, it would have made no difference. That's the point. It would be neither unprecedented (unless you count the way it was passed) nor extraordinary to overturn parts of a federal law (the Supreme Court has done it many times). And a court that restrains democracy is not an activist court, it is a rare court that is functioning properly.

Obama should, as a matter of tradition, know that a small unelected group upholding individual liberty is a huge improvement over a mob chipping it away. Alexander Hamilton argued that the court protects (or should protect) the deeper will of the people, because the Constitution represents our overarching values. Newly instituted laws, on the other hand, could often reflect transitory emotions, lack of knowledge, or flawed politicians. Hamilton also argued that federal courts would be the "least dangerous" branch. In this he was surely wrong. The Supreme Court, in its present design, is a single judge away from only occasionally caring about enumerated powers or ignoring them altogether. Democrats have fought hard to undo safeguards against direct democracy, attaching a morality to a process that can do both good and bad. Democracy allows rhetoric, false empathy, and emotion to pummel rational thinking—so it's no wonder so many politicians thrive in it. The Supreme Court, however, should rise above democracy, not give in to it. That's the point.

But it rarely does. In the end, the Supreme Court's decision turned out to be an example of judicial activism when it transformed what was a "mandate" into a "tax," though no tax existed in the law. In June of 2012, the Supreme Court upheld the health insurance mandate as a valid tax, and thus within Congress' tax and spend powers. It was a huge victory for Obamacare and the president. I was there for the reading decision, and as he neared, I was somewhat surprised to see Supreme Court Chief Justice Roberts defensively declare that the courts shouldn't be in the business of protecting citizens from the consequences of their political decisions. It is, in fact, its job. A small unelected group upholding individual liberty is a vast improvement over the opposite. This is why Alexander Hamilton argued that the court protects (or should protect) the deeper will of the people, because the Constitution represents our overarching values. Newly instituted laws, on the other hand, could often reflect fleeting emotions, lack of knowledge, or flawed politicians.

Hamilton also claimed that federal courts would be the "least dangerous branch." In this he was surely wrong. Even if the individual mandate is struck down by the Supreme Court this summer (and it seems to me that there is some premature celebration on the right), you might want to remember this: the court is a single judge away from only occasionally caring about enumerated powers or ignoring them altogether.

There are other destructive, and somewhat paradoxical, positions that defenders of democracy take. On the left these days, for instance, there is a widespread notion that limiting free speech will help preserve it. Many American believe that the principled and high-minded political debates that we supposedly engaged in for centuries are now over. Civility is lost! Apparently, there is no better way to corrode "democracy" than by allowing defenseless voters to have unlimited exposure to free speech. Ever since the Supreme Court's *Citizens United v. Federal Elections Commission* decision removed limits on independent spending by corporations and unions, pundits and politicians have lamented the end of democracy's purity. Super PACs, after all, can raise or spend as much as they'd like, and worse, they can say anything they want. What we need is legislation dictating the limits of "legitimate" political speech and money so we can all focus again.

The IRS scandal, which was unprecedented targeting of conservative political groups by the taxing agency during the 2012 election, for example, wasn't incidental to this administration as much as it was an intuitive extension of the paranoia the left has about unfettered political expression. Democrats, after all, hadn't been merely accusing political opponents of being radicals the past four years; they'd been accusing them of being corrupt, *illegitimate* radicals. The president endlessly argued that these unregulated groups were wrecking the process at the behest of well-heeled enablers rather than engaging in genuine debate.

Heck, some of these funders may even be foreign nationals! Senators called for investigations. The *New York Times* editorial board (and others) advocated the cracking down by the IRS on conservative dissenters and getting to the bottom of the anarchy. How can Americans function in a society in which anyone can speak out or fund a cause without registering with the government first? Why wouldn't the IRS—a part of the executive branch, lest we forget—aim its guns at conservative grass-roots groups during an election in which the president claimed that a corporate Star Chamber was "threatening democracy"? Even if we concede, for the sake of discussion, that Republicans are, generally speaking, unrepentant conspiracy-mongering obstructionists who've been duped by Ayn Rand devotees and their big oil money, shouldn't those groups have the right to declare themselves nonpolitical entities practicing "social welfare" just like every other political group? Most observers now say yes, but it sure hasn't sounded that way for much of the past four years.

Back in 2009, the administration was so preoccupied with Fox News (the only news network one could reasonably call the opposition) that top-ranking administration officials—including Anita Dunn, Rahm Emanuel, and David Axelrod—made a concerted effort to delegitimize its coverage. This was also unprecedented. Not long after that effort, Attorney General Eric Holder decided to spy on a Fox journalist who was reporting on leaks—shopping his case to three separate judges, until he found one who let him name reporter James Rosen as a co-conspirator in a crime of reporting the news.

When Senator Dick Durbin (D-IL), was asked about the possibility of passing a media "shield law" to curb this sort of abuse in the future, he replied, in part: "We know it's someone who works for Fox or AP, but does it include a blogger? Does it include someone who's tweeting? Are these people journalists and entitled to constitutional protection?" In the shadow of these attacks, the Senate majority whip is troubled that there may be too many protections for speech rather than too few. That is quite remarkable—and, these days, quite unsurprising. When you value the virtuousness of democracy over rights guaranteed by the Constitution, this is what happens.

The comedian Stephen Colbert brought a lot of attention to the plague of "money in politics"—first by starting his own super PAC and then by "exploring" a bid for the White House before the 2012 elections. Colbert then, cleverly, handed his PAC to fellow comedian Jon Stewart, satirically excoriating the idea that PACs and candidates don't coordinate. (They don't need to, as ideologues can always implicitly follow each other's lead.) He did a wonderful job exposing the deep absurdity of our campaign finance system. Not once did Colbert wonder why citizens have to ask permission from government to spend their own money supporting candidates and political parties. Not once did he wonder why a nation that supposedly values free speech allows government to limit the amount of money individuals or groups can spend on engagement in politics.

Of course, Colbert doesn't need a super PAC. Those who run Comedy Central—or Fox News or CNN or any publishing house— are free to spend as much as they'd like producing politically motivated shows or books or websites. They can hire on-air talent that explicitly or implicitly endorses positions and parties. Newspaper corporations regularly endorse candidates. Yet if you and twelve of your friends wanted to back a candidate, you would have to report to a government agency. Nothing says freedom like filling out paperwork. *Washington Post* columnist Richard Cohen probably put it best when he wrote: "I am comfortable with dirty politics. I fear living with less free speech." Cohen, though, is in the minority. Polls show that Americans support these kinds of limits on free speech— including the reversal of the *Citizens United* decision. So complaining about super PACs and *Citizens United* is a political safe zone.

Remember, though, that implicit in the crusades of campaign reform activists is a belief that voters are gullible, hapless, and easily manipulated. Which is often true. But isn't it strange that those peddling "democracy" have so little faith in those who mete it out? Now, I don't have much faith in democracy, but money doesn't make politics dirty; politicians make politics dirty. The least a free nation can do is allow its citizens to hear—or ignore—all we can before we make our terrible decisions on Election Day. You may remember that the Supreme Court's *Citizens United v. Federal Election Commission* decision centered around the ability of a corporation to air a documentary critical of then-candidate Hillary Clinton. In her first case as solicitor general for the Obama administration, in fact, current Supreme Court Justice Elena Kagan went so far as to argue that the federal government should be empowered to ban books if Washington deems that they amount to "political electioneering."

The political theorist Anthony Downs, in his groundbreaking work *An Economic Theory of Democracy*, argues that voters will intuitively gather around the middle of the ideological spectrum, especially in a two-party system. American representative democracy is sustainable only if there is a broad ideological consensus among its citizens. In a two-party system, each party comprises a relatively broad range of ideological positions, discouraging extremism in the various factions. When there are only two major parties, Downs observes, each party tends over time to imitate the other. The dynamic is quite different in multi-party parliamentary systems, in which each party gravitates toward a more distinct position and consensus becomes more difficult. The historical political stability of our two-party system distinguishes American government from that of most of Europe, the Middle East, and Latin America.

In our system, as the divergence between the left and right grows and both sides become more rigid, increased congestion in Washington is a natural, and most helpful, condition to bring us back to an equilibrium. Yet the idea that gridlock is a curse is virtually the consensus position. Since Republicans took control of the House of Representatives in 2010, liberal pundits and politicians have called conservatives "hostage takers,"[3] "anarchists," "political terrorists,"[4] and so on, for failing to propel the majority-approved agenda of Democrats, who not only won two presidential elections rather convincingly but also frequently lead in polls on an array of issues. The conventional wisdom in the media is that minority Republicans are attempting to "nullify" laws by using the institutions of a republic to stop a majoritarian monopoly on legislation. They have embraced these anti-democratic abuses for various reasons—racist, reactionary, or radical, we don't always know—but the outcome is the same: progress is thwarted.

During a 2013 flare-up in the Affordable Care Act debate, CNN's Anderson Cooper got into a fascinating argument with the conservative congressman Raul Labrador of Idaho.[5] House Republicans were trying to derail the implementation of Obamacare, and Cooper, often one of the more thoughtful cable news personalities, pointed out that President Obama was twice elected on a platform of universal healthcare. How could anyone try to overturn or defund a law that was simply dripping with democratic legitimacy?

Labrador retorted that Republicans had won the House in 2010 and 2012 in elections that were also acts of democracy—a more diffused and localized democracy, to be sure, but a representative nonetheless. Cooper refused to accept this argument. "You're nullifying two presidential elections and you're nullifying the vote of Congress because you don't like it," the CNN host insisted.*

In this instance, Labrador might have thought to ask Cooper a few theoretical questions we could all learn from: If you really believe in democracy, why is a decision of Congress from 2009 more important than a contrary decision from 2011 or 2030 or 2000 or 1942—or for that matter, five minutes ago? Are Congressional decisions irreversible? And do you believe that a law passed by democratic institutions can still be wrong, immoral, unethical, or unfair? Does the minority then have a duty to its own constituents to slow the completion of the majority's wishes through any legal means available?

A policy's democratic credentials don't make it sacrosanct. The Defense of Marriage Act was passed by a vote of 342 to sixty-seven in the House and eighty-five to fourteen in the Senate.[6] Activists, politicians, big money donors, and the media relentlessly attacked the law for years despite the overwhelming popular support with which it had been passed. Would Anderson Cooper demand the same unquestioning respect for DOMA to which Obamacare is supposedly entitled? Americans twice elect a president who championed the Iraq War, and yet progressives never stopped opposing it. In 2001, No Child Left Behind passed the House by a vote of 384 to forty-five and the Senate by a margin of ninety-one to eight.[7] Yet liberal groups and many elected officials have been trying to undermine it from the moment it became law. Are the opponents of No Child Left Behind attempting "nullification," or do they have a right to use the means our republican system provides to ameliorate what they believe is a bad law?

---

* I would quibble with appropriateness of the term "amnesty," which is an offer of forgiveness for criminal activity. The extension of citizenship, on the other hand, is a reward—not to mention a moral hazard.

A follower of Aristotle or Burke would argue that this is exactly what a minority should do for the good of the nation. The tension between conservatism and progressivism allows the country to move slowly and steadily forward, rather than lurching. Both sides can't be right on any given issue, but they both serve a purpose. From this perspective, the Republican opposition to Obamacare is not pointless obstructionism. It is the healthy counterbalance to progressive activism (or perhaps hyperactivism). What liberals in their frustration condemn as "gridlock" is moving our political focus to the middle of the ideological spectrum. The legislative congestion that we see is the system's organic reaction to attempts to move too far and too fast to the left. Liberals, in other words, are mistaking stability for gridlock.

When the Republican House "anarchists" held their ground in the debt-ceiling debate of 2010, the result—the spending cuts known as "sequestration"—was a genuine compromise. Neither side was completely happy with the package, but according to the Congressional Budget Office, sequestration trimmed the federal budget by 1.5 percent[8]—one of the most successful spending cuts in the past two decades.

The conservative House, then, is one of the few institutions preserving the republic, even if it's completely by accident. After a two-year binge of unbridled left-wing legislation—Obamacare (passed without a single vote from the minority party), the Dodd-Frank financial regulation act, and nearly a trillion dollars of "stimulus" spending on an array of liberal hobbyhorses—the Constitution's checks and balances finally kicked in. President Obama, who was so eager to "fundamentally transform" the United States, must now pursue his agenda through executive orders, court challenges, and regulation by fiat. He can inflict a lot of damage that way, as we're discovering, but the progressive orgy in Congress is over.

One of the major problems with democracy is that it often turns on the very mechanisms that provide the stability necessary for self-rule. Americans, who believe in the sanctity of democracy, also believe in "getting things done." Both Republicans and Democrats like to measure success by how many laws they pass. Both Republicans and Democrats piously lecture their opponents about their responsibility to "take care of the people's business." The rarely acknowledged truth, however, is that, most of the time, *doing nothing* is more constructive than *doing something*. That's probably why conservative Congresses tend to be unpopular.

The art of "doing nothing" has been perfected by the divided Congress that has sat since 2011. That year, after the Republicans won control of the House of Representatives, Congress passed only ninety bills, the first time since 1995 that fewer than 125 bills were passed.[9] Only sixty-one bills made it into law in 2012,[10] and fifty-two in 2013. For some of us, that's tremendous progress. "These statistics make the 112th Congress, covering 2011–12," *USA Today* reported, "the least productive two-year gathering on Capitol Hill since the end of World War II. Not even the Eightieth Congress, which President Truman called the 'do-nothing Congress' in 1948, passed as few laws as the current one, records show."

"Is this the kind of government our Founders envisioned?" demanded an irate Roger Simon in *Politico*[11] when congressional Republicans refused to surrender to the executive branch on spending and a government shutdown loomed. The answer is yes, it probably is. In our constitutional republic, the president doesn't get to dictate unilaterally which legislation is negotiable. In fact, the president shouldn't even *have* a "legislative" agenda.

The constitutional checks on his plans to "fundamentally transform" the United States have been irksome to President Obama. His rule by executive order has betrayed an arrogance unequaled by any president in memory. He circumvented Congress on college loans and mortgages; he directed the Justice Department not to defend the Defense of Marriage Act; he used the Environmental Protection Agency to impose energy policy that Congress wouldn't pass; he involved the United States in military action in Libya (the right kind of warring, apparently) without congressional consent; he made "recess" appointments without a recess; and that's just for starters.

Barack Obama hasn't issued an unusually large number of executive orders, but he has employed them to bypass Congress on important issues that were under debate. Even if you agree with granting eight hundred thousand young illegal immigrants a reprieve from deportation[12]—as I do—an executive end-run around a perfectly legitimate legislative deadlock should alarm everyone. It hasn't. When one person enjoys an abundance of democratic political capital, he can quickly transform it into an authoritarian mandate. Just ask the Senate majority leader, Harry Reid, who has been advancing an anti-republican argument for years. The president, Reid explained, is free to craft immigration policy unilaterally because "we've tried to do that for years, and we can't because they won't let us." This is simply an anti-American argument.

Obama is not the first president to exercise his executive powers aggressively. But no one has argued so bluntly that he was using these powers as an extension of democracy. "We can't wait for Congress to do its job," he declared. "So where they won't act, I will. We're going to look every single day to figure out what we can do without Congress." In a speech on climate change in 2013, Obama explained, "Our founders believed that those of us in positions of power are elected not just to serve as custodians of the present, but as caretakers of the future. And they charged us to make decisions with an eye on a longer horizon than the arc of our own political careers. That's what the American people expect. That's what they deserve." Wrapping himself in the mantle of the Founders (whose moral authority he seemed to be discovering for the first time), Obama seized control of environmental policy from Congress and the states and imposed his agenda on the entire country. Centralized democracy thus undermined the local democratic process—in the name of the people.

The urge to rationalize this kind of abuse is a permanent and dangerous feature of partisan democracy. The *New York Times* editorial page editor, Andrew Rosenthal, for example, offered an age-old excuse for the personal rule of Barack Obama by executive order: "Context and intent make all the difference."[13] No, they make no difference. That's why we have constitutional safeguards against this kind of one-man government, even when the policies imposed enjoy the approval of the *New York Times*. The left claims there is an unprecedented level of obstructionism in Washington (failing to note that perhaps there is an unprecedented level of terrible legislation in need of obstruction), which necessitates alternative methods. Americans should be far more comfortable with obstructionism than executive unilateralism. Unfortunately, that isn't the case.

While Barack Obama was growing weary of Republican opposition in the House of Representatives, his fellow Democrat Harry Reid was running out of patience with his Republican colleagues in the Senate, who relied on the filibuster to block the appointments of certain judges and officials. When Senator Reid's party was in the minority, he warned that weakening the Senate filibuster would "destroy the very checks and balances our founding fathers put in place to prevent absolute power by any one branch of government."[14] With his party's attainment of a Senate majority, however, Reid's reverence for the Founding Fathers' checks and balances faded, and he began to threaten Republicans with a rule change—the so-called "nuclear option"—that would eliminate the filibuster from Senate debate. Without the filibuster, only fifty-one votes, not a supermajority of sixty, are required to confirm a nominee or pass legislation. With no support from the minority party necessary, the door is open to governance along far more partisan and ideological lines.

Senator Jeff Merkley, an Oregon Democrat, offered a justification for this rupture with the tradition of the upper house. Republicans, he charged, "are going to disable the executive branch if a minority of the Senate disagrees with or dislikes the president the people elect. It's come into a realm where it's just unacceptable because if the executive branch can't function, then the nation can't respond to the big challenges it faces."[15]

Since the election of Barack Obama, the Democrats, supposedly powerless to face America's "big challenges," had passed a nearly trillion-dollar stimulus, a restructuring of the entire healthcare system, far-reaching immigration legislation that would create tens of millions of new citizens, and a tangled overhaul of financial regulation. The president had also appointed two fervently liberal Supreme Court justices with no meaningful opposition. It is a record of political accomplishment unequaled since the Johnson administration. Republicans must be the most inept obstructionists of all time.

One-party government, moreover, is not necessarily more efficient at enacting major legislation, as David Mayhew shows in his book *Divided We Govern*. Legislative accomplishments, he argues, are a product of the mood of the electorate rather than the effectiveness of legislators. Dwight Eisenhower, Ronald Reagan, and George W. Bush, for example, all working with a Congress at least partly controlled by their own party, signed nine major laws apiece in a two-year period. Richard Nixon, working with a Democratic Congress, signed twenty-two major laws in 1969–1970. Lyndon Johnson and the Democratic Eighty-Ninth Congress broke the pattern, producing twenty-two major laws in the session that unleashed the Great Society. Gerald Ford signed fourteen important bills into law in 1975–1976, also with a divided government.[16]

Merkley's justification for abolishing the filibuster, then, was transparently political. More important, his argument is incompatible with the Founders' view of government. Though each party detests the filibuster when it is in power, progressives hold an enduring contempt for it because they hold an enduring contempt for federalism in general. A more majoritarian process makes it easier to take advantage of fleeting public sentiments to ram through comprehensive "reforms," forcing even the most reactionary states to toe Washington's line.

Many thought that Reid's threat to abolish the filibuster was a bluff. It wasn't. In November 2013, he insisted that Republicans allow up-or-down votes on three appointments to the court of appeals for the District of Columbia circuit, appointments that would tip the balance decisively in the Democrats' favor on the court that would eventually determine the success of Obama's attempt to rule by regulation. When Republicans refused, Reid changed the Senate rules and abolished the filibuster for votes on presidential appointments.[17] As a practical matter, this is a change that cannot be reversed. No majority will offer to restore the filibuster to its opponents, and the future of the filibuster for legislation is now in doubt. It's true that the Constitution itself says nothing about the filibuster, which is a creature of Senate tradition. But the tradition is, for the United States, an ancient one, one of the last vestiges of the Founders' vision of the Senate as a representative body insulated from the blasts of the democratic storm.

The Constitution's blueprint of government is beautifully inefficient. So we should do our best to preserve the tangled checks and balances. The constitutional goals of this government are justice, tranquility, the common defense, general welfare, and liberty, not high legislative output. George Friedman, the chairman of the global intelligence company Stratfor, said it best: "It was a government created to do little, and what little it could do was meant to be done slowly."[18]

For short-term partisan gains, Harry Reid and others like him have inflicted dangerous structural damage to the dam that holds back direct democracy, and such damage is almost never repaired. Without the constitutional mechanisms that diffuse democracy, it accelerates, and power is further centralized in Washington.

Perhaps the least understood and most unpopular of the Constitution's impediments to direct democracy is the electoral college.[19] In every presidential election the media report the "popular vote" won by each candidate, but the Constitution recognizes no such thing. A tally of the national popular vote gives us a gauge of public sentiment nationwide and it encourages the winner to claim an inflated mandate, but it does not determine who will be president.

That's the job of the electoral college, established by Article II, Section 1, of the Constitution and modified in 1804 by the Twelfth Amendment. Each state appoints a "number of electors equal to the whole number of senators and representatives to which the state may be entitled in the Congress." It is those 538 electors who vote for the president and vice president, each elector's vote being determined by the decision of the popular vote in his state. A majority (270 votes) is required for election. If no candidate receives a majority, the House of Representatives chooses the president. It is possible for the electoral college system to produce a president who did not prevail in the popular vote nationwide. That has happened only four times—in 1824 (John Quincy Adams), 1876 (Rutherford B. Hayes), 1888 (Benjamin Harrison), and 2000 (George W. Bush).

The electoral college might be the most obviously "anti-democratic" feature of the Constitution, and most Americans therefore detest it, dismissing it as an anachronism that contradicts the sacred principle of "one man, one vote." According to a 2013 Gallup poll, 63 percent would abolish the mechanism.[20] Sentiment was even stronger at the height of the counterculture in 1968, when 80 percent of those polled wanted to abolish the electoral college. The figure was 67 percent in 1980.

Aversion to the indirect election of the president is nothing new. In the nineteenth century Senator Charles Sumner of Massachusetts characterized the electoral college as "artificial, cumbrous, radically defective and unrepublican." Larger states have always felt hampered by it. In 1970, a movement to overturn the Twelfth Amendment—with support from Richard Nixon—probably would have succeeded had it not been for a filibuster by senators from smaller states. (A filibuster preserving the electoral college—I wish I could have seen it live!) Alexander Keyssar of Harvard's Kennedy School of Government and the author of *The Right to Vote: The Contested History of Democracy in the United States*, has opined, "If we were writing or revising the constitution now, we would almost certainly adopt a rather simple method of choosing our presidents: a national popular vote, followed by a run-off if no candidate wins a majority. We applaud when we witness such systems operating elsewhere in the world. Perhaps we should try one here."[21]

We do? We should? Who applauds those foreign systems? While we admire other cultures, few Americans want to adopt the parliamentary system of other nations. What country has enjoyed the consistently peaceful turnover of power between political parties that we have— an achievement all the more impressive in a country as massive and diverse as the United States? The constitutional counterbalances to democracy have fostered the moderation necessary for our happy political track record.

The electoral college compels Washington to attend to the needs of all Americans. Candidates must focus on more states rather than fewer and think about the needs of people who do not live in densely populated areas. Wyoming, with a population under six hundred thousand, can be as critical in a presidential election as California, with a population of over 38 million.[22] The electoral college fosters restraint and national cohesion. It protects large swaths of the nation from being bullied. It encourages the federal government to craft policies that meet the needs of Colorado as well as New York. It also should remind us that smaller states have industries and functions that make them more important than their population suggests—the agriculture sector of a state, for instance. Smaller states are laboratories for new ideas. If they are coerced to think and act like the larger states, the nation loses valuable resourcefulness, imagination, and brainpower.

Without the electoral college, New York, California, and a handful of other states will decide the presidency, and politicians will have an incentive to run up the vote in those states by making ever larger promises to them.

Nevertheless, the electoral college remains our constitutional stepchild. It would surely be a distant historical memory if the Constitution were not so difficult to amend. But a clever effort has emerged to eliminate the electoral college without a constitutional amendment. The National Popular Vote[23] Interstate Compact, supported by progressive groups around the country,[24] would replace the Framers' prescription for the election of the president with a nationwide popular referendum.

When a state joins the NPV compact, it agrees to award all its electoral votes to the candidate who won the most popular votes nationwide, *even if that candidate did not carry that state's vote*. The agreement takes effect only when states representing 270 electoral votes have joined the compact. If 270 electoral votes are pledged to the winner of the national popular vote, then that candidate is guaranteed victory, regardless of what the electoral vote might otherwise have decided. As of July 2013, nine states and the District of Columbia, representing 136 electoral votes, had joined the compact.

Most educated Americans recognize that federalism is the best way to restrain democratic power. So why are so many of the ideas that embody federalism so unpopular? The rise of the Tea Party in 2008 gave new life to an idea that had been percolating for some years in libertarian circles: repealing the Seventeenth Amendment, which replaced the Constitution's original provision for the election of senators by state legislatures with the direct popular election of the upper house of Congress. A return to the earlier practice would give state governments a far stronger voice in Washington.

Yet a Huffington Post poll in 2013 found that 71 percent of voters think senators should be elected by direct popular vote, and 64 percent believe the Seventeenth Amendment should remain in place.[25] Opinion makers treat repeal of the Seventeenth Amendment as absurd and radical. Cal Jillson, a professor of political science at Southern Methodist University, offered a characteristic opinion:

"We've moved away from the idea of white male elites guiding the authority to the idea that every citizen should have an equal role."[26]

Setting aside the puerile racial component of his comment (which, as a matter of logic, has nothing to do with the argument), Jillson should know that federalism augments diversity in government by giving a voice to minorities who could not be heard in a direct democracy. Despite popular bromides about everyone's vote "being heard" in a democracy, the losing vote is never heard.

My favorite take on the Seventeenth Amendment debate was offered by Alex Seitz-Wald, a thoroughly liberal but often interesting commentator, who was then a political reporter at Salon.com. He begins,

> America, we're told from a young age, is all about democracy, and democracy is all about choosing whom you want to be your representatives and holding them accountable. This seems like an entirely uncontroversial idea, but a surprising number of Republican politicians would like to do away with this right, and return the country to an older era when Americans didn't directly elect their representatives in Washington.[27]

Every single word, thought, and contention in the above paragraph is wrong—or should be. I will concede many of us are taught that America "is all about democracy," and that's why ideas that would diminish majoritarian domination are so hard to discuss. Yet we are lucky still to have numerous anti-democratic features of our government. We certainly don't take a vote to see if the First Amendment should apply to everyone. Federal judges enjoy lifetime tenure to protect them from democratic pressure. Most people actually value anti-democratic aspects of government, yet they recoil from the principle behind them.

It was the early-twentieth-century progressives, the precursors of today's leftists, who were responsible for the Seventeenth Amendment. It is no mere coincidence that an exponential growth of federal spending followed the adoption of that amendment. And the Founders believed that state governments were better equipped than the national government to understand and deal with the desires of their citizens.

———————

Democracy doesn't reflect real life. Not really. We are far better at getting along outside of Washington than in it. It is funny, though, how often those who view society through the prism of politics and democracy are amazed that in an open society we do in fact get along. The "New American Center," a survey commissioned by *Esquire* and NBC News, revealed an explosive finding: we're not having a civil war after all. As if we needed more proof, Obama pollster Benenson Strategy Group and Romney pollster Neil Newhouse of Public Opinion Strategies have discovered that a majority of us have congealed into centrists—just millions of rational and logical realists looking for solutions and otherwise minding our own business. Or, as NBC News puts it:

> Culturally, the center could be the butt of any joke in America, with lives that encompass Duck Dynasty and NPR, baby arugula and all-you-can eat Fridays. The center includes suburban mothers, rural working class men, rich

city-dwelling business-people and relatively disaffected
young people.

Welcome to America, people! And though this poll tells us absolutely
nothing new about our own views, it tells us plenty about conventional thinking within Washington and the media. And though the
"our nation isn't as divided as we think" story is apparently a counterintuitive novelty for those who consistently portray half the country as off-their-rocker, musket-toting troglodytes, the reality is that
most people think about politics only occasionally, and even then in
the abstract. That's great news. No doubt you go through your entire
day interacting with a diverse assortment of Americans—of different
sexes, races, and ethnicities—without ever asking what they think
about capital gains tax rates or the debt ceiling.

   Now, if we continue to make a national political issue out of
everything imaginable—healthcare to education to how little we
exercise—that may change. But we're not there yet. In fact, if we're to
believe the results of the *Esquire*-NBC poll, we have to concede that
the nation isn't as right-wing as the Tea Party or as liberal as the self-
styled standard bearers of the rational center, the modern-day Democratic Party. Americans support offshore drilling (81 percent),
ending affirmative action in hiring and education (57 percent), and
limiting abortion in the third trimester. Only one in four Americans
supports reforms that offer a path to citizenship for illegal immigrants. We should therefore conclude that the major political party
representing the right has been profoundly incompetent. The most
striking problem with the poll, though, is the poll. Our ideological
views aren't always sophisticated, but they aren't always a template.
I've encountered a so-called Tea Party activist who thinks a bailout

of student loans is a super idea and a progressive journalist who could only be described as a gun nut. Democracy instills a simplicity to our views that creates intractable political battles that we often work out rather easily in the real world.

CHAPTER 12

THE FAILED GOD

*A great deal of democratic enthusiasm descends from
the ideas of people like Rousseau, who believed in democracy because
they thought mankind so wise and good that everyone deserved a
share in the government. The danger of defending democracy on those
grounds is that they're not true.... I find that they're
not true without looking further than myself. I don't deserve a share
in governing a hen-roost, much less a nation.... The real reason
for democracy is.... Mankind is so fallen that no man can be trusted
with unchecked power over his fellows. Aristotle said that some
people were only fit to be slaves. I do not contradict him.
But I reject slavery because I see no men fit to be masters.*
—C. S. LEWIS, PRESENT CONCERNS

*Laws alone cannot secure freedom of expression; in order
that every man may present his views without penalty there
must be a spirit of tolerance in the entire population.*
—ALBERT EINSTEIN

George W. Bush often argued that humanity is hard-wired to strive for freedom. "It is the policy of the United States to seek and support the growth of democratic movements and institutions in every nation and culture, with the ultimate goal of ending tyranny in our world," he declared in his inaugural address in 2005.[1] In spreading democracy around the world, Bush continued, the United States would "persistently clarify the choice before every ruler and every nation—the moral choice between oppression, which is always wrong, and freedom, which is eternally right."

The notion that all men yearn for freedom and that spreading democracy is the way to satisfy that yearning seems obviously true to most Americans, though we may disagree about the best way to spread democracy. Why on earth wouldn't everyone want to be "free" just like us? But maybe freedom isn't quite as important to everyone else as we would like to believe. The late political philosopher Kenneth Minogue put it best in his last book, *The Servile Mind*: *How Democracy Erodes the Moral Life*, observing that the history of both "traditional societies and totalitarian states of the twentieth century suggested that many people are, in most circumstances, happy to sink themselves in some collective enterprise that guides their lives and guarantees them security."[2] Handing people democratic institutions is no more a guarantee of freedom than invading their nations and coercing them to accept our way of life.

As we've noted, liberty—liberalism, freedom, virtue, and morality—is the condition for democracy, but the reverse isn't always true—as Jews living in late-1930s Germany or blacks in the Jim Crow South would have known. As John Dunn, author of *Democracy*: *A History*, and an admirer of majoritarian institutions concedes, "Democracy in itself, as we have seen, does not specify any clear and definite structure of rule. Even as an idea (let alone as a practical expedient) it wholly fails to ensure any regular and reassuring relation to just outcomes over any issue at all."[3] History, moreover, has rarely been hospitable to individual autonomy, and even when people are given the opportunity to expand their liberty they often choose not to. Even here in the United States, both the right and the left, in different ways, are susceptible to the temptation of preferring security over freedom. Most of us are amenable to small doses of authoritarianism because it makes us feel a bit safer from crime, alcohol, Wall Street, pornography, terrorism, or the vagaries of the economy. Not all forms of coercion are the same, but incremental losses of freedom add up. And remarkably enough, most of the time these intrusions don't come from some powerful overlord; we bring them on ourselves through our democratic institutions.

Many people will argue that freedom *is* the ability to live in a stable and secure world. What use is liberty, after all, if you can't afford health insurance or feel safe on the street? In any case, if we, who live in a nation with a deeper tradition of liberalism than any other, wrangle over the definition of freedom, imagine how difficult it is for everyone else in the world.

In 2002, Steven Levitsky of Harvard and Lucan A. Way of the University of Toronto foresaw the problem with assuming that people who are offered democracy will want it. In a study for the National Endowment for Democracy they wrote, "Particularly in Africa and the former Soviet Union, many regimes have either remained hybrid or moved in an authoritarian direction. It may therefore be time to stop thinking of these cases in terms of transitions to democracy and to begin thinking about the specific types of regimes they actually are."[4] If that's true, the citizens of these formerly totalitarian countries are exercising their newfound democratic powers in favor of a society that is less than free.

There are many examples of countries moving in an authoritarian direction with the assistance of popular elections. Post-Soviet Russia has seen rampant abuses of freedom. Authorities regularly intimidate activists and the press. The Russian government controls the country's three main television channels, and at the end of 2013 President Putin replaced the national news agency with a new and more compliant version.[5] In recent years the Kremlin has imposed limits on protests, criminalized libel, and censored political material on the internet. It has banned the work of nongovernmental organizations (typically aimed at fostering more transparency in government), frozen the assets of human rights groups that receive funding from U.S. citizens, and jailed the political opposition. Occasionally a dissident dies of poisoning.

And the Russian government is more popular than it's been in a long time.[6]

The reversal of once promising liberal reforms in Russia is not the result of an undermining of democracy. It happened with the full consent of the electorate. In Russia's first presidential election, in 2000, Vladimir Putin, who had previously been made prime minister, won 53 percent of the vote. In 2004, he won 71 percent of the vote. In 2008, his lackey Dmitry Medvedev also won in a landslide. In 2012, Putin returned to the presidency in a landslide election with a parliament dominated by members of his party, giving him virtually one-party rule. There don't appear to be any democrats waiting in the wings, either. The Communist Party leader, Gennady Zyuganov, came in second place with 20 percent of the vote.[7] In nearby Uzbekistan, Islam Karimov, the country's only president since independence in 1991 and whose rule has seen widespread torture, murder, corruption, press censorship, and roundups of political dissidents, won his last election with 88 percent,[8] down from his previous high of 91 percent. In Kazakhstan, Nursultan Nazarbayev has also been in control since 1991, winning 96 percent of the vote in 2011. Democracy isn't exactly a competitive enterprise, as three of Nazarbayev's opponents endorsed him.

These stories are no surprise. According to a 2011 Pew Research study of global attitudes about democracy, support for freedom among citizens in the former Soviet Union has waned rather than increased. In places like Lithuania and Russia, more people still approve of a multi-party political system than disapprove, but that opinion had precipitously dropped since 1991:

> When asked to assess the current state of democracy, few in the former Soviet republics surveyed say they are satisfied with the way it is working in their country. In Ukraine, just 13% offer a positive assessment, while 81% are dissatisfied with the way democracy is working. About a quarter in Russia (27%) and Lithuania (25%) are satisfied, while 63% and 72%, respectively, express discontent.[9]

Moreover, around 60 percent of Ukrainians and Russians told researchers that they would rather have a strong leader than a democratic government. When asked which is more important, democracy or a strong economy, over 70 percent of Russians, Ukrainians, and Lithuanians said a strong economy.

If the people polled made any distinctions between "democracy" and a fully functioning tolerant, constitutional government, I would probably agree with them. Democracy can't always work. The problem is that the authoritarians who win power in these nations are often worse than the mob. Curiously enough, one of the most successful efforts at creating a free state in the region is not a "democracy" at all. As the journalist Joshua Kucera explains:

> If democracy can have any claim to success in the former Soviet Union, its best case is Georgia, whose 2003 Rose Revolution, led by the U.S.-educated Mikheil Saakashvili, brought dramatic reforms and a sharp geopolitical turn toward the West. Saakashvili's affection for the United States was reciprocated: President George W. Bush visited the country in 2005 and famously called it a "beacon of liberty."
>
> But "democracy" was never quite the right word to describe what Saakashvili was trying to implement. His successes, while undeniable, are better thought of as progress toward modernization or good governance. Saakashvili's youth (he became president at 36), fluency in English, and rhetorical embrace of "democracy" cleverly disguised what was in effect a more enlightened version of the strongman model favored in many parts of the former Soviet Union.[10]

Saakashvili had reformed entire institutions in Georgia, made government more accountable, less corrupt and headed toward progressive policies that would likely have been supported by most Americans. But those reforms were not instituted democratically. Imperfect as things turned out, the reorganizations and reforms implemented by Saakashvili would have been nearly impossible in your ordinary democracy, much less a nation that had a long history of corruption and prevailing attitudes against such change.

The situation elsewhere in the world isn't much better than in the former Soviet Union. South American democracies invariably skew toward state-controlled economies. In Venezuela, Hugo Chavez tried violently to overthrow President Carlos Andrea Perez in 1992 and eventually came to power through open elections in 1999. After gaining control of all the country's institutions, nationalizing industry, stifling free speech, and wrecking the economy, Chavez and his socialist successors have won nearly every election since. In Ecuador, the authoritarian president Rafael Correa makes arbitrary arrests and undermines free expression, but he becomes only more popular. The ruling parties of Bolivia and Nicaragua likewise attack liberal freedoms every day, yet they win elections by comfortable margins. Some of these regimes' support undoubtedly is the result of corruption and force, but it is indisputable that many, if not most, of their citizens supported them.

Why do people willingly surrender freedom? Some value safety and stability over liberty. Many people—some of them right here in the United States—fear that self-rule is a form of anarchy. Some lack a tradition to implement the changes. Some are impatient. Some turn to the state because they are destitute. Many are swayed by an array of cultural forces—ethnic and racial divisions that we here in America can't fully understand. Others are bound by an inherited culture that includes no tradition of individual freedom. In most of the places where democracy has been tried it has failed. It cannot succeed in a cultural vacuum.

In July 2003, the British prime minister Tony Blair told a joint session of the U.S. Congress, "There is a myth that though we love freedom, others don't; that our attachment to freedom is a product of our culture; that freedom, democracy, human rights, the rule of law are American values, or Western values; that Afghan women were content under the lash of the Taliban; that Saddam was somehow beloved by his people; that Milosevic was Serbia's savior." In the early 2000s, this brand of idealism was popular. Milosevic, incidentally, *was* the elected president of Serbia from 1989 to 1997 and the elected president of the Federal Republic of Yugoslavia from 1997 to 2000. It makes him no better. And while I suspect that Afghan women do not enjoy living under the lash, it is nevertheless true that the Islamic world's conception of "freedom" is quite different from ours. *How* different is a question for religious scholars to hash out. But the idea that democracy is Afghan women's avenue to freedom is a delusion.

In their coverage of the "Arab Spring"—the wave of demonstrations, protests, and revolutions that swept over much of North Africa and the Middle East at the end of 2010—television reporters, talking heads, politicians, academics, and average Americans regularly and carelessly talked about "democracy" and "freedom" as if they were the same thing. It's not the only mistake they made, but for our purposes it is certainly the most instructive. Most of us wish the Muslim world the best in shedding its dictatorships and theocracies and building liberal institutions. But operating on the assumption that free elections will inevitably produce benevolent and well-functioning governments is a dangerous myth. We know that dictators can make their people suffer while they pursue wars of aggression or brutal ideological crusades, but no one would ever repeatedly *elect* governments that treat them so poorly—right? When the choice is between guns or butter, a fully enfranchised population is assumed to have a strong preference for butter.

So the West has long been obsessed with the spread of democracy in the Middle East, believing that it will alleviate the pressures that lead to terrorism and internal oppression, bringing stability to this vital, oil-rich region. It's an article of Western faith that democracies do not make war against each other (though the history of the twentieth century suggests otherwise). This is easily extended to the proposition that robust democracy would defuse the terrorism bomb by giving dissenters a more productive outlet for their energies.

Democracy is also thought to nourish an appetite for international connections, a hunger to assume a position of respect in the world community. Everyone wants the benefits of international trade. Free people consume vast amounts of information, which flows from every corner of the world in the age of the internet. Would an electoral majority perpetually support the sort of outlaw government that makes a pariah of its nation? Yes, actually. Until genuine political, economic, and cultural liberty are established, democracy is unlikely to offer anything more than a simulacrum of legitimacy for an oppressive regime.

Throughout the tragic history of the Middle East, across much of the Muslim world, we have seen that the triple play of political, economic, and cultural freedom is very difficult to make. To be brutally honest, it hasn't happened *anywhere* outside the United States and its key European allies. Perhaps the most intractable delusion of Western foreign policy is that tyranny is not natural. We underestimate how easily people can be oppressed, for generations on end. Liberty does not spontaneously follow upon the universal franchise.

The postwar Middle East got off on the wrong foot, as Western powers drew all sorts of cockamamie borders based on their own political needs. There are few lines on a map of the Middle East that someone has not tried to wash away with blood over the past hundred years. Unfortunately, the political and cultural residue of the old imperial occupiers was quickly wiped away. The European powers, in the throes of post-colonial self-loathing, conspired with Arab nationalists to expunge the Western values that are indispensable for the success of republican government. Whatever the Middle East gained in cultural self-esteem was more than outweighed by the resulting decades of political chaos.

It is common for the Western intellectual to assume that his nation's values are invalid beyond its borders and suspect within them. The rest of the world responds to this half-hearted, guilt-ridden "advertising" for the fruits of democracy and concludes the goods are inferior. To cite a famous observation of Osama bin Laden's, when people see a strong horse and a weak horse, they naturally prefer the strong one. This applies to *cultural* strength as well as military. Who wants to emulate societies that hate themselves?

Yet the vital and uniquely Western combination of political, economic, and cultural freedom must be secured *before* democracy can take root. Allowing all citizens to vote in free and fair elections is only a third of the recipe, and it won't work without the other two ingredients. The sort of government that sweeps into power without a firm foundation of economic and cultural liberty quickly loses its appetite for holding free and fair elections. The Muslim Brotherhood government of Mohammed Morsi in Egypt, which was democratically elected after the overthrow of Hosni Mubarak, quickly turned despotic and had to be overthrown in turn by the military. Egypt simply isn't prepared to deal with open elections because many of the participants will use elections to consolidate theocracy or tyranny. Little seems to have changed in that country since ten biblical plagues failed to win pharaoh's respect for minority rights. A recent Pew poll finds that 54 percent of Egyptians believe that women and men should be segregated in the workplace, 82 percent believe that adulterers should be stoned, 84 percent believe that apostates from Islam should face the death penalty, and 77 percent believe thieves should be flogged or have their hands cut off. An environment like that makes Chicago politics look like a garden party.

The grim political conditions of post-Mubarak Egypt were easy to predict: the Muslim Brotherhood and the even more radical Islamists of the Salafist movement were far better organized than democratically-minded reformers could manage on short notice. Given the opportunity to vote for someone other than the generally pro-Western strongman Mubarak, Egypt promptly voted for an anti-Western Islamist strongman, who proved even less capable of handling the business of government. Unfortunately for the United States, the inept and tone-deaf foreign policy of the Obama administration left all sides united primarily by their dislike of America.

Egyptian politics might have overcome the desperate poverty and seething resentments that render it so toxic if Hosni Mubarak and his chums had been a bit less corrupt. A prosperous and growing economy with high employment, in which all citizens feel like stakeholders, is more likely to bring the type of peaceful and stable republic the West would like to do business with, the sort of republic in which it might find some reflection of its own values. Starving people do not hold elevated political discussions. Throughout the Muslim Middle East, unfortunately, royal families, brutal dictators, and kleptocrats keep a tight grip on national riches. There is no democracy, but there are also few if any enlightened monarchs, who might provide a transitional government on the way to democracy.

Economic liberty calls for, and leads to, many desirable social qualities, which make a populace more likely to embrace stable elected government. Property rights, honest law enforcement, a stable currency, business-friendly licensing and regulation, private ownership of capital—these constitute the atmosphere of independence and responsibility that shifts the balance of power into the hands of the people, creating a wide and deep prosperity in which most citizens participate. Most of the Middle East has never shared the English-speaking world's evolution to constitutional monarchy or republican government. The Islamic world has yet to produce its Magna Carta or Declaration of Independence. It still waits for its native-born John Locke and does not seem eager to import the works of the original.

Islam, unfortunately, has proved almost universally friendly to authoritarian regimes. And so the third leg of the Middle East's democratic stool, cultural liberty, is broken. Western intellectuals prize tolerance—at least in theory—and would rather shop at Walmart than appear to criticize the Islamic faith. But it's distressingly easy to make the case that Islam is generally hostile to cultural liberty, especially in nations that follow Islamic law as a matter of official policy. This is not to say that every follower of Islam is a bigot. But Muslim countries simply do not share our moral understanding of freedom.

It requires stubborn and willful blindness to look across the Middle East and deny that Islamic rule is generally rough on religious minorities, including those who belong to the "wrong" sect of Islam. Much of the conflict in Middle Eastern nations is between Sunni and Shi'a Muslims. It's even rougher, of course, to be a Christian or some other kind of non-Muslim caught in the middle of such a conflict, as the violently persecuted Christians of Syria or much-abused Copts of Egypt can attest. Our ally Saudi Arabia treats women as second-class citizens, excluding nearly half its population from any participation in political life.

To be fair, we must acknowledge that Muslims in Egypt stood up for their Coptic Christian neighbors on many occasions, including the wave of unrest that swept Mohammed Morsi and the Muslim

Brotherhood out of power in 2013. Islam's resistance to pluralism and cultural liberty is not insurmountable. But it hasn't been surmounted yet, and cultural liberty—including religious liberty—is an indispensable component of stable democracy. All three of the great liberties must be present in abundance.

The need for political liberty is obvious, but it's a serious error to believe the other two will achieve sufficient strength merely because freedom of the vote has been secured. Cultural liberty may be the most easily overlooked, and yet most essential, of the three freedoms necessary for democracy. That's because cultural liberty reflects how citizens view *each other*. They must respect one another's beliefs to the extent of defending the expression of ideas the majority disagrees with. Only then can people trust each other enough for economic liberty to thrive, unleashing the full power of capitalism and commerce. People who loathe and distrust each other are unlikely to join forces to create a profitable enterprise or to engage in mutually beneficial honest trade? They are more likely to call upon the power of government as protection from one another, or, more dangerously, the majority will insist that government deploy its power to subdue despised minorities.

That view of government pleases authoritarians, and unfortunately it conforms easily to Islamic law's many injunctions to subdue and dominate unbelievers. The ears of tyrants are always listening for the call for cultural oppression. When a critical mass of citizens are busy hating the "other," they don't have much energy or time left over for hating the local despot. A divided populace is willing to settle for less from its government, as long as the enemies of the people feel heavy boots upon their throats. By no means are these strategies unique to the Middle East, but they seem to work especially well there. An atmosphere of restricted cultural liberty is toxic to democracy, which above all else must accept the proposition that "all men are created equal"—otherwise, why should they all enjoy an equal vote? How can there be free and fair political organization without the freedom of expression? How can a subdued and oppressed minority feel as though it has a voice in the affairs of the nation?

And what sort of true "election" can be held in a captive state where everyone is afraid to speak up against the ruling dictatorship? What typically results from the introduction of "democracy" into a society deprived of cultural and economic liberty is a sham election in which the dictator is "reelected" in perpetuity with 95 percent or more of the "vote." Saddam Hussein of Iraq used to hold such "elections." His Baath Party ideology was imported from Syria, where it holds sway to this day. Baathism began as a form of Syrian nationalism, eventually merging with socialist theory to become the sort of ideological virus that invades every corner of the citizen's life. The Pan-Arabist ideology that came to be championed by Egypt's Gamal Abdel Nasser actually grew out of Baathism. Pan-Arabism was a sort of unified nationalism that sought to fuse many Arab states into a single entity that would rival the greatest nations of the West as a world power, working under the direction of a single mighty dictator. Just about every strongman in the Middle East, from the late Saddam Hussein to the more recently departed Muammar Gaddafi, has auditioned for the role since Nasser's death.

Such romantic illusions of nationalism are yet another mechanism for suppressing the three great liberties, turning politically inconvenient minorities into hated "others" and propping up gruesome, inept governments long beyond the point where a free populace would vote them out of office. Nationalism is usually the last excuse cited by every Middle Eastern despot who refuses to step down; some of Gaddafi's final statements on the subject of his personal identification with Libyan destiny were positively delirious.

Effective democracy requires citizens to have a clear view of the difference between the enduring identity of a nation and the transitory authority of a government that deserves to get its walking papers at the ballot box if it doesn't manage its affairs properly. People cannot be expected to vote against a ruler who presents himself as the incarnation of the national spirit, especially since there are usually patrols of unsmiling men with guns and cudgels roaming the streets to remind everyone that voting against such a sacred leader is sinful. Nationalism, the political application of Islamic law, the ancient claim to power of royal families, internal sectarian divisions, the fear of external enemies such as Israel and the Great Satan, the United States, all prevent government from assuming the appropriately *humble* posture necessary for the people to tame it with their votes. Democracy, when it's working for all the people under it, is an act of submission by the state to its people. Proud and self-righteous rulers whose power is secured by violent oppression or sanctified through religious law rarely entertain such thoughts of submission. We are a long way from genuine freedom in the world. If the past few years have taught us anything, it is that democracy is not the first step in bringing it about.

CHAPTER 13

"YEARNING TO BREATHE FREE"?

*The Americans are very patriotic, and wish to make
their new citizens patriotic Americans. But it is the idea of making
a new nation literally out of any old nation that comes along.
In a word, what is unique is not America but what is called
Americanisation. We understand nothing till we understand
the amazing ambition to Americanise the Kamskatkan and
the Hairy Ainu. We are not trying to Anglicise thousands of
French cooks or Italian organ-grinders. France is not trying
to Gallicise thousands of English trippers or German prisoners of war.
America is the only place in the world where this process, healthy
or unhealthy, possible or impossible, is going on. And the process,
as I have pointed out, is not internationalisation. It would be truer to
say it is the nationalisation of the internationalised. It is making
a home out of vagabonds and a nation out of exiles.*
—G. K. CHESTERTON, *WHAT I SAW IN AMERICA*

*All the problems we face in the United States today
can be traced to an unenlightened immigration policy
on the part of the American Indian.*
—PAT PAULSEN

I mmigration infuses our nation with a healthy dose of diversity and new ideas. It reinvigorates American culture. It shaped our character—as a nation and as individuals—and has been a vital part of our success. There is ample evidence that immigration provides an economic advantage, helping to keep social programs solvent by increasing tax revenue and economic activity.

But for immigration to work, immigrants must assimilate culturally. They must learn to speak the language of their adopted nation, they must be able to take care of themselves and their families without government assistance, they should tend to intermarry with their new countrymen, and, most importantly in my view, they must accept the governing philosophy of their new home—especially when the people of that new home define themselves by ideas rather than conventional racial or ethnic ideas.

While significant numbers of immigrants do bring with them a strong sense of family and a work ethic we admire, many also retain notions about the role of the state that do not fully comport with the American interpretation of individual freedom—especially before they have been here long. Certainly it is understood that this takes time. This slowness to appreciate America's political tradition wouldn't be a problem if it weren't for two things: democracy and big government. So while politicians and pundits reflexively assert that immigration in any form and in any numbers is beneficial for this nation of immigrants, we ought to evaluate the cost of welcoming millions of new citizens into the country while government, and thus democracy, continues to grow exponentially.

The Founders believed that citizenship was more than an inherited title or a license bestowed on a man by the government. It does not signify membership in a race but adherence to a set of principles. Proponents of immigration and increased diversity should understand that when multiple ethnic, religious, and racial groups cohabit a single country, it is their philosophical cohesion that makes them a nation. So should we liberally offer citizenship to people who do not fully understand the American ideal of liberty and justice for all? Are large-scale immigration and democracy even compatible? Might we create a massive new voting bloc that changes the way the state functions? Can immigrants whose first act on our soil was breaking the law be expected to revere the rule of law? What will happen to American enterprise when millions of first-generation citizens grow up knowing nothing but dependency on the state? Could there be an influx of immigrants great enough to change forever the ideological complexion of the United States?

Despite what you may have heard, the United States is hardly stingy about allowing immigrants into the country. According to the Census Bureau, 13 percent of America's population in 2010 was born elsewhere—the highest proportion since 1920, and almost three times the percentage of 1970. The government reports that 40 million foreign-born persons live here, including illegal immigrants.[1] How many illegal immigrants are there? The Pew Research Center puts the number at around 11 million.[2] No other country in the world is as generous.

I want to emphasize that it is not immigration but democracy that undermines the assimilation of newcomers. Our educational system fails to convey to its students—native-born as well as immigrants—the knowledge and culture that have traditionally defined Americans. And the welfare state robs immigrants of self-sufficiency, one of the foundations of a strong citizenry.

Constant pressure from a coalition of big business, big government, and big religion compels Washington politicians to support wide-ranging immigration "reform" that includes amnesty—

extending citizenship to most of the 11 million people living illegally in America.*

When Gallup asks Americans what the country's most pressing problems are, "immigration" barely makes an appearance among the responses.[3] When asked, though, most Americans support the nebulous idea of immigration "reform." As news stories have dependably informed them for years, the immigration system is "decades-old" and "broken." And in a democracy, if something happens to be "old," it is assumed to require "change"—never mind Chesterton's warning that we should understand *why* something exists before we change or eliminate it. Our immigration system is probably no more "broken" than the welfare system, the Social Security, Medicare, and Medicaid systems, or any other system run by the government, yet it is unique in its urgent need of reform.

The American habit of romanticizing immigration makes it the perfect issue for populists. In 2012, by executive order, the Obama administration ignored Congress and began halting deportations and offering work permits to students who were brought to the country illegally as children by their parents—the would-be beneficiaries of the still unpassed "Dream Act." "They pledge allegiance to our flag," Obama explained. "They are Americans in their hearts, in their minds, in every single way but one: on paper."[4] That's surely true for some, and surely not for others, but immigration policy seems specially shielded from rigorous debate. Obama's immigration policy highlights the conflict between the "compassion" arguments of the left and the "rule of law" arguments of the right. Many conservatives opposed amnesty for the children of illegal immigrants not only

---

* I would quibble with appropriateness of the term "amnesty," which is an offer of forgiveness for criminal activity. The extension of citizenship, on the other hand, is a reward—not to mention a moral hazard.

because of the extra-legislative manipulation by which the president bestowed it but because it rewards bad behavior. It was also an example of how a president took advantage of the power he acquired through democratic victories to impose his policy unilaterally ("this is the right thing to do for the American people," as he put it).

Yes, most immigrants pledge allegiance to our flag, but some have a tough time conforming to American cultural norms, and others have an even tougher time accepting our traditional political ideals. In a 2011 Pew Research Center poll of Hispanics, only one in four described himself as a "Latino," a slim majority preferred to identify themselves with the country of their origin. Only one in five described himself as "American." In the early 2000s, a longitudinal study of five thousand children of immigrants from seventy-seven countries revealed that after four years of American high school, students were less likely to identify themselves primarily as Americans and more likely to self-identity by their parents' home country or by ethnic category.[5]

More recently, John Fonte and Althea Nagai of the Hudson Institute published a detailed study of immigrant assimilation, which focused on civics and belief systems.[6] They discovered a large "patriotic gap" between native-born citizens and immigrant citizens on issues of attachment to this country and civic knowledge. In his bestselling novel *Choke*, Chuck Palahniuk expresses the traditional view of immigrants' loyalty: "The truth is, immigrants tend to be more American than people born here." Actually, the truth is that native-born citizens have far stronger patriotic attachment to the United States than naturalized citizens. Here were some of Fonte's and Nagai's key findings:

- By 21 percentage points (65 to 44), native-born citizens are more likely than naturalized immigrants to view

America as "better" than other countries, as opposed to "no better, no worse."

- By about 30 points (85 to 54), the native-born are more likely to consider themselves American citizens rather than "citizens of the world."
- By 30 points (67 to 37), the native-born are more likely to believe that the U.S. Constitution is a higher legal authority for Americans than international law.
- By roughly 31 points (81 to 50), the native-born are more likely than immigrant citizens to believe that schools should focus on American citizenship rather than ethnic pride.
- By 23 percentage points (82 to 59), the native-born are more likely to believe that it is very important for the future of the American political system that all citizens understand English.
- By roughly 15 points (77 to 62), the native-born are more likely to believe that there is a unique American culture that defines what it means to be an American.
- By 15 points (82 to 67), the native-born are more likely than immigrant citizens to support an emphasis in schools on learning about the nation's founding documents.

I imagine that the respondents might have felt pressure to give the answers to these questions that they thought Americans would want to hear. But taking the responses at face value, they contradict the conventional wisdom about immigrants. We trust that everyone who makes the effort to come here—leaving behind everything he knows and sometimes even risking his life—is pining to be the best American citizen he can be. This is simply not so. When respondents were asked, for instance, if it was "very important," "somewhat important," "not that important," or "not important at all" for the future of the political system for citizens to speak and read English, 82 percent of the native-born Americans responded that both speaking and reading English were "very important" to preserve the nation's democratic institutions. Only 59 percent of the naturalized citizens thought so. We may hope that these attitudes will change with time. But democracy could instead encourage the normalization of bad behavior, and creating 8 million new citizens overnight is one way of doing it. A monolithic new voting bloc of that size could be politically destabilizing.

A 2012 Gallup poll found that Hispanic voters born outside the United States believe, by a whopping 61-to-22 percent margin, that government should "do more to solve our country's problems."[7] That opinion might sound innocuous enough to many Americans, but when a three-trillion-dollar-a-year government has its hands in everything from our education to our healthcare to our light bulbs to the ingredients in our doughnuts, we might ask what more there is for government to do. Only 37 percent of the registered voters surveyed in the same poll gave that answer. We can't say precisely how illegal immigrants would vote if they could, but considering how legal immigrants vote, it is not difficult to guess. The Pew Research Center's National Survey of Latinos found in 2012 that 31 percent of Latino immigrants who are not U.S. citizens or legal permanent residents (so likely illegal) identify as Democrats and only 4 percent as Republicans. Thirty-three percent of them claim to be political independents, 16 percent identify with another political party (a far higher rate than among natural-born citizens), and 15 percent "don't know" or didn't answer the question.[8] Democrats are understandably eager to add such a gigantic and reliable bloc of voters to the American electorate, but they shouldn't be surprised that the rest of us have a problem with an immigration process that would permanently shift the balance of power in American politics.

Some argue that Hispanic and other immigrants vote disproportionately Democratic because that party supports a pathway to citizenship for illegal immigrants, and indeed this has become the conventional wisdom among the media and establishment Republicans. But what if the leftward tilt of immigrants is in fact more deeply rooted? What if their political choices when they come here reflect the political cultures of the countries from which they have come?

Paul Mirengoff's analysis of the Hispanic vote in the presidential elections from 1980 through 2012 suggests that Republican positions on immigration have had little effect on the party's ability to attract Hispanic votes:

> In 1986, President Reagan signed an amnesty bill into law. In the next election, his vice president received only 30 percent of the Hispanic vote, down from the 37.5 percent Reagan had averaged in the pre-amnesty days. Hispanic voters did not punish Clinton in 1996 for signing IIRIR [The Illegal Immigration Reform and Immigrant Responsibility Act, which was opposed by immigrant groups] into law. In fact, the Republican share of the Hispanic vote dropped to 23 percent, its lowest during the nine-election period. It should be noted, though, that Clinton had threatened to veto punitive measures that would have barred the children of immigrant children from public schools. Republicans may also have felt some backlash among California's Hispanic voters for supporting Prop 187 two years earlier.

The Republican candidate won the following percentages of the Hispanic vote in the presidential elections from 1980 through 2012[9]:

- 1980: 38 percent
- 1984: 37 percent
- 1988: 30 percent
- 1992: 29 percent
- 1996: 23 percent
- 2000: 36 percent
- 2004: 43 percent
- 2008: 32 percent
- 2012: 28 percent

As Mirengoff points out, in 2008 John McCain, who was the leading advocate for an immigration bill that would have granted amnesty, received only 32 percent of the Hispanic vote. Mitt Romney, who declared his support for "self-deportation" of illegal immigrants in 2012, won only 4 percent less of the Hispanic vote; his 28 percent was the median and, roughly, the mean share for Republicans in the last nine races. In the thirty-two-year period that Mirengoff studied, Hispanics increased from about 1.5 percent of the electorate to nearly 12 percent. There seems to be no correlation between immigration policy and the Hispanic vote. For Republicans, improving their share of the Hispanic vote is a long-term project that hinges on compelling economic ideas, not pandering. But if millions of Hispanic voters are suddenly added to the rolls by amnesty, it is likely that the Democratic Party will consolidate its claim on their support.

It's not only Hispanic immigrants who consistently vote with the left—almost all newcomers do. Asians, who have recently passed Hispanics as the largest group of new immigrants to the United States,[10] are a particularly puzzling case. According to a Pew study, more than 61 percent of adult immigrants from Asia hold a bachelor's degree, double the percentage of other immigrants.[11] They tend, therefore, to achieve high levels of success in the United States. Pew found that they are more "satisfied than the general public with their lives, finances and the direction of the country, and they place more value than other Americans do on marriage, parenthood, hard work and career success." Assimilation and achievement on such a scale would not suggest to most observers monolithic support for the Democratic Party. But Asian Americans supported Barack Obama over Mitt Romney in 2012 by an estimated 72 percent to 26 percent. When asked with which party they identified, 46 percent responded they were independent, 36 percent claimed Democratic affiliation, and 17 percent were Republican. The same thing goes for Indian Americans, another large and successful immigrant group. Their median household income of $88,000 is more than $40,000 above the national mean. But according to a 2012 Pew poll, 65 percent of Indian Americans identify with the Democratic Party and only 18 percent with the Republican Party, making Indian Americans more aligned with the Democratic Party than any East Asian group. Though Asians and Indians have strong traditional values, they are far more likely to support a statist economic policy.

Most immigrants, however, are not well off. They start off poor in their home countries, and our growing welfare state offers them incentives to come here. It is unlikely that poor people won't take what the government offers them, and not vote for the party that offers it. The economist Milton Friedman argued that open immigration and a welfare state could simply not coexist harmoniously. The dramatic expansion of the welfare state makes the addition of 8 million new citizens over the next ten years—the Congressional Budget Office's projection if immigration reform were to pass—a terribly costly prospect.[12] If there's one thing the War on Poverty excels at, it's keeping people poor. A government that sells dependency as freedom—and that's been the Obama administration's theme—and massive immigration is a bad combination, no matter how good the intentions of immigrants might be. This is why Friedman also said, a bit less famously, that immigration in a welfare state was "only good so long as it's illegal."

The question before our country is whether the status quo is healthier for the economy than creating millions of new citizens who will be thrown into the welfare system and the arms race of goodies that politicians will offer them. Is it healthy for democracy to appeal to immigrants by promising that government will do more? Wasn't it a Democrat who once upon a time urged us, "Ask not what your country can do for you"? The idea that many immigrants, once they are offered dependency, won't partake of it seems risible.

One way to guess how the welfare system would be burdened by legalizing substantial numbers of illegal immigrants is to look at the "public charge" status. The term does not appear in the text of the most recent immigration reform legislation—and there's a very good reason for that. The U.S. Citizenship and Immigration Services defines "public charge"—which has been a part of immigration policy (often ignored) since the 1950s—as any individual who is likely to become "primarily dependent on the government for subsistence, as demonstrated by either the receipt of public cash assistance for income maintenance, or institutionalization for long-term care at government expense."[13] In the past, immigrants would promise not to become dependents of the state. Even with "public charge" status in place, too many newcomers turn to the state for subsistence. In 2012, a Republican Senate Budget Committee study found that of 10.37 million applications for immigrant and non-immigrant visas processed by the State Department in fiscal year 2011, only 0.068 percent were rejected as "public charge"—and most of those rejections were later overturned.

Los Angeles County officials expected illegal immigrant parents to receive $650 million in welfare benefits—food stamps and other programs—for their native-born children in 2013. About one hundred thousand children of sixty thousand illegal immigrant parents receive about $54 million in welfare payments each month—$20 million in California benefits and $34 million in food stamps—up from $53 million in July 2012.[14] Would these habits change once those receiving the benefits can vote for those providing them?

As long as immigration "reform" promises an electoral bonanza for their party, Democrats will relentlessly pursue amnesty with a "path to citizenship" for illegal immigrants. And Republicans— deluded into thinking that immigrants to the modern American welfare state will assimilate as earlier generations did, or cowed into submission by the fear of seeming uncompassionate—might actually cooperate. The real problem with our immigration debate is its focus on voting rights, which exacerbates the problem of combining a mass democracy with a welfare state. The greatest benefit of citizenship shouldn't be a financial claim on your new countrymen enforced by the electoral power of the Democratic Party. It's the privilege of settling in a stable country rich in opportunities for the industrious and enjoying the protections of our Constitution.

DON'T VOTE!

*The difference between a democracy and a dictatorship is that
in a democracy you vote first and take orders later;
in a dictatorship you don't have to waste your time voting.*
—CHARLES BUKOWSKI

*Why do the people humiliate themselves by voting?
I didn't vote. No! Because I have dignity.... If, at a certain moment,
I had closed my nose and voted for one of them, I would spit on my
own face.*
—ORIANA FALLACI

Voting is not a sacramental rite. Democracy is not a religion. And notwithstanding the sanctimonious lecturing of many politicians and pundits, in a democracy, the more people that vote the less each vote matters. That's math.

At the Pew Research Center for the People & the Press, they like to categorize voters into a number of distinct groups.[1] There are "regular voters"—adults who are registered to vote and tend to participate in nearly every election they can. They constitute roughly a third of the adult population of the United States. Next, there are the "intermittent voters," or Americans who are registered to vote but vote less regularly than "regular voters" and usually participate only in what they view as the most consequential elections. They make up around 20 percent of the population. Then there are "unregistered adults"—Americans who say they are not registered to vote and who obviously do not vote and do not care to vote. They account for 22 percent of the population.

Why don't people vote? For the reasons you might expect. A few years back the Caltech/MIT Voting Technology Project studied that question[2] and found that the most common reasons given were that people were too busy or had a scheduling conflict (17 percent), had an illness or disability (15 percent), had no interest in the process (13 percent), or had a dislike for candidates or issues that are being offered (13 percent). Six percent couldn't figure out the voter registration process, 3 percent could not find a polling place that was convenient, 3 percent had transportation problems, and 0.2 percent could not get to the polls because of inclement weather.

The failure of Americans to vote is the occasion of perpetual lamenting in Washington. It's such a big problem that we see an increasing number of people arguing that Americans should be coerced to vote—whether they are educated enough to do so, whether they have any desire to do so, or whether they have any interest in the candidates available to them. Strong-arming the citizens of a free nation to participate in democracy—which, as we've discussed, equates with "liberty" and "freedom" to most people—is laughably contradictory. Or perhaps it tells us a bit about how democracy is viewed by its most ardent proponents.

What, you might ask, if my non-voting is itself a political position? Not voting is a choice, after all. Too bad, says Peter R. Orszag, a former director of Obama's Office of Management and Budget. Not only should there be social pressure to vote, it should be compulsory. "The U.S. prides itself as the beacon of democracy, but it's very likely no U.S. president has ever been elected by a majority of American adults,"[3] Orszag asserts. And who is to blame for this? "It's our own fault—because voter participation rates are running below 60 percent, a candidate would have to win 85 percent or more of the vote to be elected by a majority."[4] Others agree. William Galston, a scholar at the Brookings Institution, argues that forcing everyone to vote would temper political "polarization." Activists and partisans have a disproportionate influence in government, while moderates and unaffiliated voters are always on the outside. If voting were compulsory, then our government would be responsive to groups less inclined to participate in the political process—the young, poor, and uneducated. If we forced everyone to vote then everyone would become more interested in what was going on in Washington and educate themselves so as to make educated decisions.

There are many problems with these contentions beyond the problem of expanding democracy. For starters, it's peculiar to hear so many people who embark on careers in Washington claim that they have deep-seated moral aversions to "partisanship," which is the normal atmosphere there. The two-party system, with all its obvious faults, allows most of you to vote for some generally acceptable envoy to advocate for whatever ideological belief system you've decided on that election cycle. Though blind "partisanship" is unhealthy, there are worse fates. One of them is political unity.

If people began to pay attention when forced to participate in the process, they would, like almost everyone else, pick sides and thus expand partisanship—though the dynamics of the debate are likely to stay the same. Partisanship would become uglier, but it is unlikely that people would change their outlooks if coerced. A study called "If Everyone Had Voted, Would Bubba and Dubya Have Won?" by John Sides at George Washington University—which Orszag glosses over in his argument for compulsory voting—concludes, "Adapting and refining the approach used in earlier work on Senate elections, we simulate the impact of universal turnout on each presidential election from 1992 to 2004 and find little evidence that increased turnout would systematically transform partisan competition or policy outcomes."[5]

And ask yourself this: What's more reckless? Not voting, or voting when you know nothing about the candidates? In fact, it's amazing so many Americans vote. "Public choice" theory holds that good government policies in a democracy are an underprovided public good because of the rational ignorance of voters. Making an informed voting decision requires a lot of time that many people don't have and effort they don't want to expend. And since the probability that their votes are going to change the result of a given election is minimal, for many voters, the decision to remain ignorant and skip voting altogether is the rational one. Rational choice theorists point to this choice to explain voter ignorance and low voter turnout. The economist James Buchanan calls public choice theory "politics without romance,"[6] and Anthony Downs, who wrote the famous *An Economic Theory of Democracy* (1957), says that ignorance of political issues is logical. If turnout increases but voter ignorance stays the same, then voters are moving from rational ignorance to irrational ignorance.

Irrational choices are not confined to voting or government, but that's where those irrational choices have serious consequences for others. And what smart observers like Galston truly lament is the lack of legislative and technocratic growth in Washington. If "partisanship" is a legitimate division driven by ideology, it is perfectly healthy. Politics is a process, not an end. There can't be an end. There is no right answer or policy for everyone. Only process. Massive groups of people rarely have shared preferences or think together or deploy rational arguments as individuals do. Here is how Buchanan laid it out:

> [I disagree] with those who retain a Platonic faith that there is "truth" in politics, remaining only to be discovered and, once discovered, capable of being explained to reasonable men. We live together because social organization provides the efficient means of achieving our individual objectives and not because society offers us a means of arriving at some transcendental common bliss. Politics is a process of compromising our differences, and we differ as to desired collective objectives just as we do over baskets of ordinary consumption goods. In a truth-judgment conception of politics, there might be some merit in an attempt to lay down precepts for the good society. Some professional search for quasi-objective standards might be legitimate. In sharp contrast, when we view politics as process, as means through which group differences are reconciled, any attempt to lay down standards becomes effort largely wasted at best and pernicious at worst, even for the man who qualifies himself as expert.[7]

Democracy—even the most diffused, federalist democracy ever devised—cannot survive with a goal of doing away with debate, ugly disputes, or eternal ideological arguments, even disputes that render government impotent with gridlock. It should simply insure that those disagreements do not degenerate into violence, that most people can function freely and virtuously, and that they can pursue happiness without the government's interfering with their wishes.

Galston argues that voting would prompt more Americans to pay attention to their choices. Young people are often uninterested in politics because they don't know enough and because they've made a rational decision to focus their energies on other things. Does Galston believe that the impelled voter will run to the *Federal Register* to review daily entries to make sure he is educated about Washington? Forcing uninterested citizens to participate in democracy is like forcing sinners to go to church.

"Compulsory voting, as exists in Australia and more than two dozen other countries," Orszag tells us, will cure citizens' lack of interest. Other nations—beacons of democracy like Bolivia, the Dominican Republic, Egypt, Gabon, Mexico, and Turkey—have compulsory voting. If you skip a vote in Australia, you will pay a $20 fine and receive a tersely worded letter from the electoral commission demanding an explanation. Is Australia more stable than the United States? Are human rights there more secure? Let's concede for the sake of argument that the partisan debate that Galston and Orszag dislike is a problem. Does Australia experience less partisanship? I'm no expert, but after veering sharply to the left a few years ago, Australians in 2013 elected a conservative majority under Tony Abbott, who opposes same-sex marriage and wants to curtail immigration. (He's also a fan of constitutional monarchy.)

Eric Liu, writing in *Time* magazine, reveals the fundamental misconception behind compulsory voting:

That is why the best reason for mandatory voting has nothing to do with today's politics. It's about redeeming the central promise of American citizenship. Generations marched, fought and died for the right to vote. The least we can do now is treat that right like a responsibility.[8]

Voting is not the central promise of American citizenship. The central promise of the United States is laid out in the Constitution, which doesn't even mention the "right" to vote. At some point, primarily because of the ugly history of racism, it became taboo to argue that many Americans aren't prepared for the ballot. But I'm not talking about race, and I'm not talking about excluding anyone by force. Government shouldn't exclude anyone from voting. Only voters themselves can preserve federalism and self-government. Rather than encouraging the inattentive to vote, we should be campaigning against democratic excess. It is almost impossible, however, to imagine that happening.

Pew identifies "registered but rare voters." I probably fit in that category, though perhaps a better category for me would be "registered but does his utmost to avoid voting." There are numerous reasons I avoid the ballot. I have explained many of them here. A journalist, opinion columnist, and editorial board member, I have avoided voting for the most part as a matter of professional propriety. (Journalists need not shun voting, but they should be transparent about their voting if they're going to cover policy.) Then again, I didn't lose much sleep over it. Even if I were inclined to vote, I would rarely find a candidate worthy of support. This isn't because I hold the ballot sacred. Quite the opposite. When voting for president, I may vote for the lesser evil, but generally I throw my support behind some quixotic third-party candidate as a futile gesture of protest. I *waste* my vote on purpose. And any votes I happen to take on local elections matter even less. I've lived nearly my entire adult life in iron-clad liberal districts that offer almost no competition past the primary stages of an election. And there's nothing wrong with people clustering into ideologically congenial locales. We have the space. We used to have the federalism. Do Americans want to live with like-minded neighbors and vote for officials who represent the worldviews of those communities? God bless them. But they don't have the right to force others to live as they do.

That, regrettably, is often the point of a modern democracy. Despite what we so often hear about being a tool for self-rule, it is more often a mechanism to impose a way of life on others. Americans love to wear those "I voted" stickers on their coats. What are they telling us? That if enough of them agree they can lord it over the rest of us. We celebrate democracy even as it slowly corrodes our foundational ideals.

One organization after another makes an idol of the vote. From school-age onward, we are enjoined to "get out the vote" or "rock the vote." You must get "involved"—which nearly always entails getting involved politically. But the most morally bankrupt platitude about voting of all is "If you don't vote you don't have a right to complain."

As far as I can tell, the Constitution makes no such stipulation for democracy. Actually, it says nothing about democracy whatsoever.

ACKNOWLEDGMENTS

As a serial reductionist, I could never have begun to understand the rich philosophical history of democracy if it hadn't been for Karl Selzer's intellectual and editorial support. Also, thanks go out to David Pietrusza, John Hayward, and Teresa Mull for their valuable assistance in making this book happen.

Tom Spence's attention to detail and expertise on a wide range of topics were invaluable in making this a better book. Then again, don't blame him for any factual errors, misleading assertions, sloppy thinking, or indefensible arguments. They are all mine.

Thanks also to Harry Crocker and Marji Ross for putting the book out, and to Maria Ruhl, Amber Colleran, Katharine Mancuso, and everyone else at Regnery for their professionalism.

It's been a blast being part of The Federalist. I'm grateful to Ben Domenech, Mollie Hemingway, and Sean Davis for including me in such an exciting project—and for giving me the time to finish the book.

Many thanks also to Tucker Carlson, Charles Cooke, Tara Ross, David Yontz, Brad Cohan, Harris Vederman, and you, the people I've inevitably forgotten to mention.

Thanks, as well, go out to everyone in my family. I owe much of who I am to Mom and Dad. Adria and Leah … sorry, *this* isn't a democracy. You'll thank me later. And, most importantly, to my wife, Carla, for being supportive, loving, and understanding.

SUGGESTIONS FOR FURTHER READING

Allen, Thomas B. *Tories: Fighting for the King in America's First Civil War*.

Aquinas, Thomas. *On Kingship*. Translated by Gerald B. Phelan.

———. *On Law, Morality, and Politics*. Translated by Richard J. Regan.

Aristotle. *Politics*, in *The Basic Works of Aristotle*. Edited by Richard McKeon.

Augustine. *The City of God*. Translated by Marcus Dods.

Boorstin, Daniel. *The Americans: The Democratic Experience*.

Brague, Rémi. *The Legend of the Middle Ages*. Translated by Lydia G. Cochrane.

Burke, Edmund. *Edmund Burke: Selected Writings and Speeches*. Edited by Peter J. Stanlis.

Campbell, Angus, Philip E. Converse, Warren E. Miller, and Donald E. Stokes. *The American Voter*.

Caplan, Bryan. *The Myth of the Rational Voter: Why Democracies Choose Bad Policies*. New edition.

Chernow, Ron. *Alexander Hamilton*.

Chesterton, G. K. *Orthodoxy*.

Dunn, John. *Democracy: A History*.

The Federalist Papers.

Filmer, Robert. *Patriarcha, or the Natural Power of Kings*, http://files. libertyfund.org/files/221/Filmer_0140_EBk_v7.0.pdf.

Gilson, Étienne. *The Unity of Philosophical Experience*.

Gutzman, Kevin R. C. *James Madison and the Making of America*.

Hayek, F. A. *The Constitution of Liberty*.

Hoppe, Hans-Hermann. *Democracy—The God That Failed: The Economics and Politics of Monarchy, Democracy, and Natural Order*.

Johnson, Paul. *Modern Times*.

———. *Socrates: A Man for Our Times*.

Le Bon, Gustave. *The Crowd: A Study of the Popular Mind*.

Levin, Yuval. *The Great Debate: Edmund Burke, Thomas Paine, and the Birth of Right and Left*.

MacIntyre, Alasdair. *After Virtue*.

Mencken, H. L. *A Mencken Chrestomathy: His Own Selection of His Choicest Writing*.

———. *Notes on Democracy*.

Minogue, Kenneth. *The Servile Mind: How Democracy Erodes the Moral Life*.

Norman, Jesse. *Edmund Burke: The First Conservative*.

Plato. *Gorgias*. Translated by James H. Nichols Jr.

———. *Republic*. Translated by G. M. A. Grube, revised by C. D. C. Reeve.

Samons, Loren J., II. *What's Wrong with Democracy?: From Athenian Practice to American Worship*.

Strauss, Leo, and Joseph Cropsey, eds. *History of Political Philosophy*.

Tocqueville, Alexis de. *Democracy in America*.

————. *Letters From America*. Edited by Frederick Brown.

Walker, Jesse. *The United States of Paranoia: A Conspiracy Theory*.

Wilentz, Sean. *The Rise of American Democracy: Jefferson to Lincoln*.

Wittman, Donald A. *The Myth of Democratic Failure: Why Political Institutions Are Efficient*.

NOTES

Chapter 1

1. "Democracy," *Wikipedia*, http://en.wikipedia.org/wiki/Democracy.
2. John Adams, "Message from John Adams to the Officers of the First Brigade of the Third Division of the Militia of Massachusetts," October 11, 1798, available on beliefnet, http://www.beliefnet.com/resourcelib/docs/115/Message_from_John_Adams_to_the_Officers_of_the_First_Brigade_1.html.
3. Roger Scruton, "A Point of View: Is Democracy Overrated?" BBC, August 9, 2013, http://www.bbc.co.uk/news/magazine-23607302.

Chapter 2

1. "One-Third of Americans Believe in UFOs, Survey Says," Fox News, June 28, 2012, http://www.foxnews.com/scitech/2012/06/28/one-third-americans-believe-in-ufos-survey-says/.
2. Larry Shannon-Missal, "Americans' Belief in God, Miracles and Heaven Declines," Harris Interactive, December 16, 2013, http://www.harrisinteractive.com/NewsRoom/HarrisPolls/tabid/447/ctl/ReadCustom%20Default/mid/1508/ArticleId/1353/Default.aspx.
3. Ibid.
4. "U.S. Belief in God Down, Belief in Theory of Evolution Up," United Press International (UPI), December 22, 2013, http://www.upi.com/Health_News/2013/12/22/US-belief-in-God-down-belief-in-theory-of-evolution-up/UPI-24081387762886/.

5.   "Conspiracy Theories Prosper: 25% of Americans Are 'Truthers,'" Fairleigh Dickinson University's Public MindPoll, January 17, 2013, http://publicmind.fdu.edu/2013/outthere/.

6.   *The Mindscape of Alan Moore*, 2003.

7.   Ryan Singel, "In Troubling Economic Times, Consumers Flock to Online Psychics," *Wired*, November 8, 2008, http://www.wired.com/science/discoveries/news/2008/11/psychic_economy.

8.   James Madison, *The Writings of James Madison*, ed. Gaillard Hunt, 9 vols. (New York: G. P. Putnam's Sons, 1900–1910), available here: "James Madison to W.T. Barry," Philip B. Kurland and Ralph Lerner, eds., *The Founders' Constitution*, vol. 1, ch 18, document 35 (University of Chicago Press and Liberty Fund Web Edition, 2000), http://press-pubs.uchicago.edu/founders/documents/v1ch18s35.html.

9.   "1912 Eighth Grade Examination for Bullitt County Schools," Bullitt County History research project, Bullitt County Genealogical Society, http://www.bullittcountyhistory.com/bchistory/schoolexam1912.html.

10.   "Don't Know Much about History?" Marist Poll, July 2, 2010, http://maristpoll.marist.edu/72-don't-know-much-about-history/.

11.   "Science 2011: National Assessment of Educational Progress at Grade 8," National Center for Education Sciences, May 2012, http://nces.ed.gov/nationsreportcard/pdf/main2011/2012465.pdf.

Chapter 3

1.   Wayne Crews and Ryan Young, "The Towering Federal Register," Daily Caller, May 21, 2013, http://dailycaller.com/2013/05/21/the-towering-federal-register/.

2.   Ibid.

3.   Jayne O'Donnell and Fola Akinnibi, "How Many Pages of Regulations Are in the Affordable Care Act?" *USA Today*, October 25, 2013, http://www.usatoday.com/story/opinion/2013/10/23/affordable-care-act-pages-long/3174499/.

4.   "United Technologies/National Journal Congressional Connection Poll Topline Results Oct. 7, 2013," *National Journal*, October 8, 2013, http://www.nationaljournal.com/congressional-connection/toplines/united-technologies-national-journal-congressional-connection-poll-topline-results-oct-7-2013-20131008.

5. Louise Radnofsky, "Health Law Faces Skepticism," *Wall Street Journal*, September 16, 2013, http://online.wsj.com/news/articles/SB100014241 27887324755104579073442586768058.

6. "Kaiser Family Foundation/NBC News Survey Questions," Henry J. Kaiser Family Foundation, September 2013, http://kaiserfamily foundation.files.wordpress.com/2013/09/8489.pdf.

7. Steve Liesman, "What's in a Name? Lots When It Comes to Obamacare/ ACA," CNBC, September 26, 2013, http://www.cnbc.com/id/101064954.

8. "Kaiser Health Tracking Poll—May 2011," Henry J. Kaiser Family Foundation, May 1, 2011, http://kff.org/health-reform/poll-finding/kaiser-health-tracking-poll-may-2011/.

9. "Press Release: Consumers Don't Understand Health Insurance, Carnegie Mellon Research Shows," Carnegie Mellon University, August 1, 2013, http://www.cmu.edu/news/stories/archives/2013/august/aug1_understandinghealthinsurance.html.

10. "Half of U.S. Adults Fail 'Health Insurance 101,' Misidentify Common Financial Terms in Plans," American Institute of CPAs, August 27, 2013, http://www.aicpa.org/press/pressreleases/2013/pages/us-adults-fail-health-insurance-101-aicpa-survey.aspx.

11. University of Texas at Austin Energy Poll, September 5–23, 2013, http://www.utenergypoll.com/.

12. Adrienne Lu, "Survey: Americans Unfamiliar with the Common Core," Stateline, August 21, 2013, http://www.pewstates.org/projects/stateline/headlines/survey-americans-unfamiliar-with-the-common-core-85899499028.

13. Ibid.

14. Lloyd Vries, "Where's Iraq? Young Adults Don't Know," CBS News, May 2, 2006, http://www.cbsnews.com/news/wheres-iraq-young-adults-dont-know/.

15. "Majority Views NSA Phone Tracking as Acceptable Anti-Terror Tactic," Pew Research Center for the People & the Press, June 10, 2013, http://www.people-press.org/2013/06/10/majority-views-nsa-phone-tracking-as-acceptable-anti-terror-tactic/.

16. Matthew Boesler, "It's Crazy How Many Americans Have No Clue What Rising Interest Rates Are Doing to Their Investments," *Business Insider*,

August 21, 2013, http://www.businessinsider.com/americans-confused-about-rising-rates-2013-8.

17. Link to survey in: Walter Hickey, "A New Poll Shows Americans Don't Actually Understand Anything about the Deficit," *Business Insider*, October 9, 2013, http://www.businessinsider.com/a-new-poll-shows-americans-dont-actually-understand-anything-about-the-deficit-2013-10.

18. Ann Saphir, "With the End of Fed's QE in Sight, U.S. Public Says 'Huh?'" Reuters, September 17, 2013, http://www.reuters.com/article/2013/09/17/us-usa-fed-poll-idUSBRE98G18K20130917.

Chapter 4

1. "DoD News Briefing—Secretary Rumsfeld and Gen. Myers," U.S. Department of Defense, February 12, 2002, http://www.defense.gov/transcripts/transcript.aspx?transcriptid=2636.

2. Maggie Koerth-Baker, "Crowds Are Not People, My Friend," *New York Times*, December 18, 2012, http://www.nytimes.com/2012/12/23/magazine/crowds-are-not-people-my-friend.html?_r=1&.

3. Robert K. Goidel and Todd G. Shields, "The Vanishing Marginals, the Bandwagon, and the Mass Media," *Journal of Politics* 56, no. 3 (August 1994), http://www.jstor.org/discover/10.2307/2132194?uid=3739584&uid=2&uid=4&uid=3739256&sid=21103149767027.

4. Jan E. Leighley, ed., *The Oxford Handbook of American Elections and Political Behavior* (Oxford: Oxford University Press, 2010), 241, http://books.google.com/books?id=0PLNhGk-MlgC&pg=PA241&lpg=PA241&dq=%E2%80%9Ccharacterized+more+by+faith+than+by+conviction+and+by+wishful+expectation+rather+than+careful+prediction+of+consequences.%E2%80%9D&source=bl&ots=qAM4JjGPc7&sig=oMkW6N18t8HKO55t7KnVDrli52g&hl=en&sa=X&ei=poO0UsSbEMngsASGyIKgDQ&ved=0CDUQ6AEwAQ#v=onepage&q=%E2%80%9Ccharacterized%20more%20by%20faith%20than%20by%20conviction%20and%20by%20wishful%20expectation%20rather%20than%20careful%20prediction%20of%20consequences.%E2%80%9D&f=false.

5. Don Irvine, "Salon's Joan Walsh Attacks Liberal Pundits for Criticizing Obamacare Website," Accuracy in Media, October 23, 2013, http://www.aim.org/don-irvine-blog/salons-joan-walsh-attacks-liberal-pundits-for-criticizing-obamacare-website/.

6. "Following the Crowd: Brain Images Offer Clues to How and Why We Conform," Association for Psychological Science, press release, February 23, 2011, http://www.psychologicalscience.org/index.php/news/releases/following-the-crowd-brain-images-offer-clues-to-how-and-why-we-conform.html.

7. Wray Herbert, "So Damn Superior: Parsing Partisan Politics," Association for Psychological Science, June 14, 2013, www.psychologicalscience.org/index.php/news/full-frontal-psychology/so-damn-superior-parsing-partisan-politics.html.

8. Tom Jacobs, "America's Increasingly Tribal Electorate," *Pacific Standard*, November 1, 2012, http://www.psmag.com/politics/our-increasingly-tribal-electorate-48977/.

9. Alice Boyes, "50 Common Cognitive Distortions," *Psychology Today*, January 17, 2013, http://www.psychologytoday.com/blog/in-practice/201301/50-common-cognitive-distortions.

10. Ryan Weber and Allen Brizee, "Logical Fallacies," Purdue Online Writing Lab, March 11, 2013, https://owl.english.purdue.edu/owl/resource/659/03/.

11. "Remarks of President Barack Obama—as Prepared for Delivery Address to Joint Session of Congress," Whitehouse.gov, February 24, 2009, http://www.whitehouse.gov/the_press_office/Remarks-of-President-Barack-Obama-Address-to-Joint-Session-of-Congress.

12. Greg Giroux, "Voters Throw Bums in while Holding Congress in Disdain," Bloomberg, December 13, 2012, http://www.bloomberg.com/news/2012-12-13/voters-throw-bums-in-while-disdaining-congress-bgov-barometer.html.

13. Jeffrey M. Jones, "In U.S., Perceived Need for Third Party Reaches New High," Gallup, October 11, 2013, http://www.gallup.com/poll/165392/perceived-need-third-party-reaches-new-high.aspx.

14.   Joy Wilke, "Americans' Belief That Gov't Is Too Powerful at Record Level,"
       Gallup, September 23, 2013, http://www.gallup.com/poll/164591/
       americans-belief-gov-powerful-record-level.aspx.

Chapter 5

1.   Loren J. Samons II, *What's Wrong with Democracy? From Athenian Prac-
       tice to American Worship* (Berkeley and Los Angeles: University of Cali-
       fornia Press, 2004), 50.
2.   Augustine, *City of God*, II, 21.
3.   Ibid., II, 20.
4.   Ibid.
5.   Thomas Aquinas, I–II, q. 105, a. 1, sed contra.
6.   Ibid, respondeo.

Chapter 6

1.   George Orwell, "Politics and the English Language," George-Orwell.org,
       http://www.george-orwell.org/Politics_and_the_English_Language/0.
       html.
2.   Charles Francis Adams, ed., *The Works of John Adams, Second President
       of the United States*, vol. 8 (Cambridge University Press, 2011), http://
       www.goodreads.com/book/show/11961383-the-works-of-john-adams-
       second-president-of-the-united-states—-volume.
3.   Jamie Weinstein, "Meet 'the Colonial 1 Percent' That Created America,"
       Daily Caller, July 8, 2013, http://dailycaller.com/2013/07/08/meet-the-
       colonial-1-percent-that-created-america/.
4.   John Ferling, "Myths of the American Revolution," *Smithsonian*, January
       2010, http://www.smithsonianmag.com/history-archaeology/Myths-of-
       the-American-Revolution.html.
5.   Thomas B. Allen, *Tories* (New York: HarperCollins, 2010).
6.   Theodore P. Savas and J. David Dameron, *A Guide to the Battles of the
       American Revolution* (New York: Savas Beatie LLC, 2006).

Chapter 7

1. Garry Wills, "Edmund Burke against Grover Norquist," *New York Review of Books*, July 14, 2011, http://www.nybooks.com/blogs/nyrblog/2011/jul/14/edmund-burke-vs-grover-norquist/.

Chapter 8

1. Stanley Hauerwas, "The Virtues of Alasdair MacIntyre," *First Things*, October 2007, http://www.firstthings.com/article/2007/09/004-the-virtues-of-alasdair-macintyre-6.
2. Bertrand Russell, "The Best Answer to Fanaticism—Liberalism; Its Calm Search for Truth, Viewed as Dangerous in Many Places, Remains the Hope of Humanity," *New York Times Magazine*, December 16, 1951, http://select.nytimes.com/gst/abstract.html?res=F50C16FB3F551A7B9 3C4A81789D95F458585F9&scp=19&sq=fanaticism&st=p.
3. Mike Springer, "Bertrand Russell's Ten Commandments for Living in a Healthy Democracy," Open Culture, March 14, 2013, http://www.openculture.com/2013/03/bertrand_russells_ten_commandments_for_living_in_a_healthy_democracy.html.

Chapter 9

1. Bradley R. Schiller, "Obama's Rhetoric Is the Real 'Catastrophe,'" *Wall Street Journal*, February 14, 2009, http://online.wsj.com/news/articles/SB123457303244386495.

Chapter 10

1. Alex Fitzsimmons, "MSM Mum on Obama's ATM Gaffe," Fox News, June 15, 2011, http://nation.foxnews.com/president-obama/2011/06/15/msm-mum-obama-s-atm-gaffe.

Chapter 11

1. Adam Liptak, "Supreme Court Gets a Rare Rebuke, in Front of a Nation," *New York Times*, January 28, 2010, http://www.nytimes.com/2010/01/29/us/politics/29scotus.html.

2.   Adam Aigner-Treworgy, "President Obama: Overturning Individual
      Mandate Would Be 'Unprecedented, Extraordinary Step,'" CNN, April 2,
      2012, http://whitehouse.blogs.cnn.com/2012/04/02/president-obama-
      overturning-individual-mandate-would-be-unprecedented-
      extraordinary-step/.

3.   Jon Favreau, "House Republican Hostage Takers Are Unfit to Govern,"
      Daily Beast, September 30, 2013, http://www.thedailybeast.com/
      articles/2013/09/30/house-republican-hostage-takers-are-unfit-to-
      govern.html.

4.   Michael Tomasky, "Republicans Aren't Hostage Takers, They're Political
      Terrorists," Daily Beast, September 30, 2013, http://www.thedailybeast.
      com/articles/2013/09/30/republicans-aren-t-hostage-takers-they-re-
      political-terrorists.html.

5.   Hadas Gold, "Anderson Cooper to Rep. Labrador: CNN Isn't Fox News,
      MSNBC," *Politico*, October 8, 2013, http://www.politico.com/blogs/
      media/2013/10/anderson-cooper-to-rep-labrador-cnn-isnt-fox-
      news-174519.html.

6.   H.R. 3396 (104th): Defense of Marriage Act (one Passage of the Bill),
      govtrack.us, https://www.govtrack.us/congress/votes/104-1996/h316.

7.   Final Vote Results for Roll Call 145, No Child Left Behind Act, May 23,
      2001, Office of the Clerk, U.S. House of Representatives, http://clerk.
      house.gov/evs/2001/roll145.xml.

8.   "The Budget and Economic Outlook: Fiscal Years 2013 to 2023," Congres-
      sional Budget Office, February 2013, http://www.cbo.gov/sites/default/
      files/cbofiles/attachments/43907-BudgetOutlook.pdf.

9.   Susan Davis, "This Congress Could Be Least Productive Since 1947," *USA
      Today*, August 15, 2012, http://usatoday30.usatoday.com/news/
      washington/story/2012-08-14/unproductive-congress-not-passing-
      bills/57060096/1.

10.   "A Summary of the Record of the 112th Congress (2011–2012) of the
      United States," Congress-Summary.com, updated through January 10,
      2013, http://www.congress-summary.com/B-112th-Congress/Laws_
      Passed_112th_Congress_Seq.html.

11. Roger Simon, "The Frauds on the Hill Target Obama," *Politico*, September 30, 2013, http://www.politico.com/story/2013/09/the-frauds-on-the-hill-target-obama-97537.html.

12. Elise Foley, "Obama Administration to Stop Deporting Younger Undocumented Immigrants and Grant Work Permits," Huffington Post, June 15, 2012, http://www.huffingtonpost.com/2012/06/15/obama-immigration-order-deportation-dream-act_n_1599658.html.

13. Andrew Rosenthal, "Government by Executive Order," *New York Times*, April 23, 2012, http://takingnote.blogs.nytimes.com/2012/04/23/executive-overreach/?_r=0.

14. David D. Kirkpatrick, "After DeLay Remarks, Bush Says He Supports 'Independent Judiciary,'" *New York Times*, April 9, 2005, http://www.nytimes.com/2005/04/09/politics/09judges.html?position=&_r=2&adxnnl=1&pagewanted=print&adxnnlx=1385046641-qbLjkhz/RyRxmXQdfrgB2A&.

15. Jeremy W. Peters, "Democrats Plan Challenge to G.O.P.'s Filibuster Use," *New York Times*, July 8, 2013, http://www.nytimes.com/2013/07/09/us/politics/democrats-plan-challenge-to-gops-filibuster-use.html?pagewanted=all.

16. David R. Mayhew, *Divided We Govern* (New Haven: Yale University Press, 2005), http://yalepress.yale.edu/yupbooks/book.asp?isbn=9780300102888.

17. Paul Kane, "Reid, Democrats Trigger 'Nuclear' Option; Eliminate Most Filibusters on Nominees," *Washington Post*, November 21, 2013, http://www.washingtonpost.com/politics/senate-poised-to-limit-filibusters-in-party-line-vote-that-would-alter-centuries-of-precedent/2013/11/21/d065cfe8-52b6-11e3-9fe0-fd2ca728e67c_story.html.

18. George Friedman, "The U.S. Debt Crisis from the Founders' Perspective," *Geopolitical Weekly*, Stratfor, October 15, 2013, http://www.stratfor.com/weekly/us-debt-crisis-founders-perspective.

19. Tara Ross offers a powerful defense of the electoral college in *Enlightened Democracy: The Case for the Electoral College*, 2nd edition (Dallas: Colonial Press, 2012).

20.   Lydia Saad, "Americans Call for Term Limits, End to Electoral College," Gallup, January 18, 2013, http://www.gallup.com/poll/159881/americans-call-term-limits-end-electoral-college.aspx.

21.   Alexander Keyssar, "Do Away with the Electoral College," *New York Times*, July 8, 2012, http://www.nytimes.com/roomfordebate/2012/07/08/another-stab-at-the-us-constitution/revisiting-the-constitution-do-away-with-the-electoral-college.

22.   2010 Census Data, Census.gov, http://www.census.gov/2010census/data/.

23.   National Popular Vote is a 501(c)(4) corporation seeking implementation of popular presidential elections, http://www.nationalpopularvote.com.

24.   "National Popular Vote—Background Info," Common Cause, http://www.commoncause.org/site/pp.asp?c=dkLNK1MQIwG&b=1695007.

25.   Emily Swanson, "Even Republicans Don't Like the Right-Wing Plan to Stop Electing Senators by Popular Vote," Huffington Post, December 4, 2013, http://www.huffingtonpost.com/2013/12/04/17th-amendment-poll_n_4379842.html.

26.   David Saleh Rauf, "Talk of Repealing 17th Amendment Invades Lieutenant Governor Race," *Houston Chronicle*, October 17, 2013, http://www.houstonchronicle.com/news/politics/texas/article/Talk-of-repealing-17th-Amendment-invades-4901939.php.

27.   Alex Seitz-Wald, "Repeal the 17th Amendment!" Salon, August 16, 2012, http://www.salon.com/2012/08/16/repeal_the_17th_amendment/.

Chapter 12

1.   "Bush Pledges to Spread Democracy," CNN, January 20, 2005, http://www.cnn.com/2005/ALLPOLITICS/01/20/bush.speech/.

2.   Kenneth Minogue, *The Servile Mind: How Democracy Erodes the Moral Life*, 4.

3.   John Dunn, *Democracy: A History*, 149.

4.   Steven Levitsky and Lucan A. Way, "The Rise of Competitive Authoritarianism," *Journal of Democracy* 13.2 (2002) 51–65, http://archive.is/v4T5T.

5.   "Russian News Agency RIA Novosti Closed Down," BBC News, December 9, 2013, http://www.bbc.co.uk/news/world-europe-25299116.

6. Mark Adomanis, "Vladimir Putin's Approval Rating Isn't Actually Declining," *Forbes*, June 11, 2013, http://www.forbes.com/sites/markadomanis/2013/06/11/vladimir-putins-approval-rating-isnt-actually-declining/.

7. Timothy Heritage and Guy Faulconbridge, "Putin Wins Presidency, Opponents Allege Fraud," Reuters, March 4, 2012, http://in.mobile. reuters.com/article/worldNews/idINDEE82304920120304?i=7.

8. "Background on Islam Karimov: President of Uzbekistan, 1991–Present," Carnegie Endowment for International Peace, March 26, 2012, http:// carnegieendowment.org/2012/09/20/airpower-at-18-000-indian-air-force-in-kargil-war/fioe?reloadFlag=1.

9. "Confidence in Democracy and Capitalism Wanes in Former Soviet Union," chapter 1, Pew Research Center, December 5, 2011, http://www. pewglobal.org/2011/12/05/chapter-1-views-of-democracy/.

10. Joshua Kucera, "Voting against Freedom," *Wilson Quarterly*, Winter 2013, http://www.wilsonquarterly.com/essays/voting-against-freedom.

Chapter 13

1. "A Nation of Immigrants," Pew Research Center, January 29, 2013, http:// www.pewhispanic.org/2013/01/29/a-nation-of-immigrants/.

2. Jeffrey S. Passel and D'Vera Cohn, "Unauthorized Immigrants: 11.1 Million in 2011," Pew Research Center, December 6, 2012, http://www. pewhispanic.org/2012/12/06/unauthorized-immigrants-11-1-million-in-2011/.

3. "Most Important Problem," Gallup, January 2001–present, http://www. gallup.com/poll/1675/most-important-problem.aspx.

4. "Remarks by the President on Immigration," Whitehouse.gov, June 15, 2012, http://www.whitehouse.gov/the-press-office/2012/06/15/remarks-president-immigration.

5. Alejandro Portes and Ruben G. Rumbaut, *Legacies: The Story of the Immigrant Second Generation* (Berkeley: University of California Press, 2001), 154–57.

6. John Fonte and Althea Nagai, "America's Patriotic Assimilation System Is Broken," Hudson Institute, April 2013, http://www.hudson.org/files/publications/Final04-05.pdf.

7.   Frank Newport, "Hispanic Voters Favor Gov't Involvement to Solve
      Problems," Gallup, June 25, 2012, http://www.gallup.com/poll/155333/
      hispanic-voters-favor-gov-involvement-solve-problems.aspx.

8.   Eileen Patten and Mark Hugo Lopez, "Are Unauthorized Immigrants
      Overwhelmingly Democrats?" Pew Research Center, July 22, 2013, http://
      www.pewresearch.org/fact-tank/2013/07/22/are-unauthorized-
      immigrants-overwhelmingly-democrats/.

9.   "US Elections: How Groups Voted in 1980," Roper Center, http://www.
      ropercenter.uconn.edu/elections/how_groups_voted/voted_80.html.

10.   Kirk Semple, "In a Shift, Biggest Wave of Migrants Is Now Asian," *New
      York Times*, June 18, 2012, http://www.nytimes.com/2012/06/19/us/
      asians-surpass-hispanics-as-biggest-immigrant-wave.html.

11.   "The Rise of Asian Americans," Pew Research Center, June 19, 2012
      (updated April 4, 2013), http://www.pewsocialtrends.org/2012/06/19/
      the-rise-of-asian-americans/.

12.   Doug Elmendorf, "CBO Releases Two Analyses of the Senate's Immigra-
      tion Legislation," Congressional Budget Office, June 18, 2013, http://
      www.cbo.gov/publication/44345.

13.   "Public Charge," U.S. Citizenship and Immigration Services, http://www.
      uscis.gov/green-card/green-card-processes-and-procedures/public-
      charge.

14.   "Undocumented LA County Parents on Pace to Receive $650M in Wel-
      fare Benefits," CBS Los Angeles, September 16, 2013, http://losangeles.
      cbslocal.com/2013/09/16/undocumented-la-county-parents-projected-
      to-receive-650m-in-welfare-benefits/.

Conclusion

1.   "Who Votes, Who Doesn't, and Why," Pew Research Center, October 18,
      2006, http://www.people-press.org/2006/10/18/who-votes-who-doesnt-
      and-why/.

2.   Caltech/MIT Voting Technology Project, http://vote.caltech.edu/.

3.   Peter Orszag, "Making Voting Mandatory," Bloomberg, June 19, 2012,
      http://www.bloomberg.com/news/2012-06-19/voting-should-be-
      mandatory.html

4.   Ibid.

5.   John Sides, Eric Schickler, Jack Citrin, "If Everyone Had Voted, Would Bubba and Dubya Have Won?" *Presidential Studies Quarterly*, September 2008, http://home.gwu.edu/~jsides/bubbadubya.pdf.

6.   William F. Shughart II, "Public Choice," Concise Encyclopedia of Economics, http://www.econlib.org/library/Enc/PublicChoice.html.

7.   James M. Buchanan, *The Limits of Liberty: Between Anarchy and Leviathan*, (Indianapolis: Liberty Fund, Inc., 1999), http://www.econlib.org/library/Buchanan/buchCv7.html.

8.   Eric Liu, "Should Voting Be Mandatory?" *Time*, August 21, 2012, http://ideas.time.com/2012/08/21/should-voting-be-mandatory/#ixzz2oDcAw6b5.

INDEX